A Guidebook to Learning

ALSO BY MORTIMER J. ADLER

Dialectic

What Man Has Made of Man

How to Read a Book

How to Think About War and Peace

The Capitalist Manifesto (with Louis O. Kelso)

The Idea of Freedom

The Conditions of Philosophy

The Difference of Man and the Difference It Makes

The Time of Our Lives

The Common Sense of Politics

The American Testament (with William Gorman)

Some Questions About Language

Philosopher at Large

Reforming Education

Great Treasury of Western Thought (with Charles Van Doren)

Aristotle for Everybody

How to Think About God

Six Great Ideas

The Angels and Us

The Paideia Proposal

How to Speak/How to Listen

Paideia Problems and Possibilities

A Vision of the Future

The Paideia Program

Ten Philosophical Mistakes

A GUIDEBOOK TO LEARNING

For a Lifelong Pursuit of Wisdom

MORTIMER J. ADLER

MACMILLAN PUBLISHING COMPANY
NEW YORK

COLLIER MACMILLAN PUBLISHERS
LONDON

Macmillan Publishing Company
866 Third Avenue, New York, N.Y. 10002
Collier Macmillan Canada, Inc.

Library of Congress Cataloging-in-Publication Data
Adler, Mortimer Jerome, 1902–
   A guidebook to learning.
   List of author's works: p. ii
   Bibliography: p. 161
   1. Learning and scholarship.   I. Title.
AZ221.A35   1986   001.2   85-23778
ISBN 0-02-500340-2

Macmillan books are available at special discounts for bulk purchases for sales promotions, premiums, fund-raising, or educational use. For details, contact:

   Special Sales Director
   Macmillan Publishing Company
   866 Third Avenue
   New York, N.Y. 10022

10 9 8 7 6 5 4 3 2 1

Printed in the United States of America

Grateful acknowledgment is made to W. W. Norton & Company, Inc., and George Allen & Unwin, Ltd, London, for permission to quote from José Ortega y Gasset's The Revolt of the Masses, copyright 1932; and to Princeton University Press for permission to quote from José Ortega y Gasset's Mission of the University, translated with an introduction by Howard Lee Nostrand, copyright 1944, © renewed 1972 by Princeton University Press.

Note to the Reader

I can think of no better way to start readers off than to tell them plainly what lies ahead. This I can do most effectively by quoting here the opening paragraphs of Chapter 13.

I can imagine that some readers who have been patient and persistent enough to reach this point will be somewhat perplexed. They are likely to be wondering what all they have been through adds up to and what comes next.

That state of mind on the part of readers may help me to achieve the objective I had in mind in writing this book.

I have given in the preceding pages a survey of the state of learning in antiquity, in the Middle Ages, and in modern times. In my judgment it was necessary for readers to become acquainted with the traditional maps or charts of learning in those periods, so as to appreciate their need for clarification and their need for guidance as to the state of learning in the contemporary world. *Such guidance is not to be found in the literature of this subject.*

The contribution, which I believe this book makes, consists in providing needed philosophical insights and distinctions that enable us to lay out the geography, as it were, of the realm of learning. I venture to say that readers will find nothing comparable to it elsewhere. My reason for surveying the literature from antiquity to the present day was to allow readers to judge for themselves whether I have succeeded in my effort to throw light in dark corners. I also hope they will find the recommendations I offer in the Conclusion of this book helpful as guidelines for self-conducted learning in the mature years of their lives.

I suggest that readers examine the Contents to see what lies ahead, and that they ponder the following statement by Aristotle, which they will find again on the title page of Part Two.

It is necessary to call into council the views of our predecessors in order that we may profit by whatever is sound in their views and avoid their errors.

I think I have done what Aristotle recommends; and I hope that, by my doing so, readers will find in the closing chapters of this book the enlightenment they seek.

M. J. A.

Carisch House
Aspen, Colorado
September 1985

Contents

[ix]

Contents

[x]

Contents

[xi]

Contents

Introduction:
Who Needs Guidance
and Why

THIS book is intended for all who have gradually come to understand what young persons, still in school, college, or university, do not know and find difficult to understand. For the most part, their teachers also fail to acknowledge the point in question. It is that no young person can complete his or her education in school, college, or university for the simple reason that youth itself—immaturity—is an insuperable obstacle to becoming a truly educated human being while still young.

One's education can be begun in institutions but it can never be completed there. Only a truly mature or adult person can possibly attain the kind of education that produces generally cultivated human beings, men and women who feel at home in the whole world of human knowledge, know their way around in it, and have the kind of understanding of basic ideas, issues, and values, together with some modicum of wisdom, that everyone should aspire to possess.

A recent report on college offerings and student choices voices the complaint that the elective system with its ever-increasing specialization of courses offered and the tendency of students to choose lines of specialization that promise immediate rewards in the marketplace, has resulted in the neglect of studies essential to the general cultivation of the mind. The report insists that for the latter purpose "some things are more important to know than others."

Schooling that is general rather than specialized, liberal rather than vocational, and humanistic rather than technical, should prepare the young for continued learning in adult life, after all schooling has been completed, without which this aspiration cannot be fulfilled and this attainment achieved. While this is not the only goal of schooling, it is certainly its most important objective.

Since everyone has a natural human right to aspire to become a truly educated person in the later years of life, the kind of schooling that serves this purpose should be accessible to everyone. That is why twenty-two persons, who joined with me in recommending a radical reform in our system of basic schooling, proposed that general, liberal, and humanistic education should start at the level of basic schooling, and should be supplemented to a modest extent in our highly specialized colleges and universities.* Only in this way can *all* be properly prepared, some more than others, for the continued learning that all should attempt to carry on in adult life in order to complete their education.

Since our basic schooling up to the present is far from being the kind of schooling recommended in The Paideia Proposal, everyone stands in need of the help that this book tries to provide. If they are to become truly educated human beings, they must embark on the sea of learning in adult life.

To set out on such a voyage without charts and maps

---

* See The Paideia Proposal, 1982.

is to be without a point of departure, an appointed destination, lacking knowledge of currents, of reefs and shoals, of depth and shallows, of distances and directions.

I have called this work a guidebook precisely because it attempts to provide something like a chart or map for the journey that everyone should undertake with the hope of finally reaching the understanding and wisdom that is the beckoning goal and culmination of the effort.

In antiquity, in the great centuries of the medieval era, and in modern times up until the end of the nineteenth century, the sea of learning was mapped and charted for those who wished to venture on voyages of exploration and discovery.

Ours is the century of the knowledge explosion. We are living in what has been called the information society. We are suffering from what José Ortega y Gasset has called "the barbarism of specialization," which dismisses a generalist approach to the world of learning as amateurism. It also finds a merely alphabetical ordering of the specialized parts of knowledge more congenial than any attempt to present a general scheme for the organization of knowledge.

Whatever merits and demerits such schemes may have had in earlier centuries, they were certainly appropriate to the state of affairs that then existed. They served the purpose for which they were constructed; but they are no longer appropriate today. They are viewed by us as relics or antiques in the museum of intellectual cartography.

We must overhaul and redraft them to make them useful. Short of doing that, we are without charts or maps. No comprehensive chart or map of the vast expanse of learning that lies before us is available for our use. In this century of the knowledge explosion and in our information society it is paradoxical, to say the least, that we should lack what earlier centuries had when there was so much less knowledge to be explored and organized.

Where would anyone now turn to find a comprehensive outline of knowledge or a schematic diagram of the arts and sciences and of other disciplines as well? Certainly not to the catalogues of schools, departments, and courses in our great universities. Certainly not to most of the encyclopedias that can be found on the shelves of libraries, and sometimes in our homes as well.

Let me explain my reference to university catalogues and general encyclopedias as two prime examples of the plight we are in. They are alike in two respects: they are both alphabetically organized, and each in its own way purports to cover the whole scope of knowledge or learning.

The word "university" echoes the word "universe"— an all-inclusive whole in which everything can be found. The very word "encyclopedia" promises to provide the great circle (encyclo) of general learning (paideia) that every cultivated human being should possess.

Indications of everything to be studied and learned are there in some fashion. But in what order, to what extent, of what value, for what purpose? That is not indicated at all. Nor is there any indication of lines of connection and separation that might enable us to plot or plan different ways of starting out, carrying on, and ending up if we wish to undertake a voyage of exploration and discovery, one that, if it is begun in youth, must continue throughout adult life.

To remedy this deficiency, I propose to proceed as follows. In Part One, I will use the alphabetical ordering of subjects in general encyclopedias and the alphabetical ordering of courses in university catalogues to present the bewildering chaos that confronts us. I will supplement this by considering card catalogue systems used for organizing books on the shelves of great libraries.

In Part Two, I will report, explain, and criticize the charts and maps of learning that we have inherited from the past. Readers will see why they must be amended and extended to be of service to us today. Then, in Part Three, I will call attention to contemporary efforts to do something about remedying the encyclopedic affliction I have called alphabetiasis.

Finally, I will present, in Part Four, the indispensable insights and distinctions that give us the guidelines to learning appropriate for us today. With these distinctions in mind, I think I can turn the chaos we face into a more orderly picture, one that will enable me to suggest an itinerary for a lifelong pursuit of wisdom. That I have attempted to do briefly in the Conclusion.

PART ONE

ALPHABETIASIS:
FROM A TO Z

CHAPTER 1

The Merits and Demerits of Alphabetical Arrangements

NOT all languages have alphabets, but the Indo-European languages that do have them confer certain benefits upon the peoples that speak these languages.

The most obvious purpose to which alphabets have been put to use is in the arrangement of large assemblages of items, such as the names in a telephone book, the words in a standard dictionary, the entries in an index, and the cards in a library catalogue. Their alphabetical arrangement provides an easy mode of access for anyone who wishes to find a particular item the initial letter of which is known.

An alphabetical ordering of items facilitates all look-it-up-to-find efforts. In most of the examples mentioned above no other ordering would serve that purpose, or serve it as well. In fact, any other ordering of the words in a dictionary or the entries in an index would amount to randomness.

The reason for this is that one cannot find, applicable to these materials, any principles or criteria for assorting, relating, and ordering them. No inherent intelligible connection exists between one item or set of items and another.

One other type of ordering is similar to alphabetizing an assemblage of items. That is a chronological ordering, which is useful, for example, in making a list of recommended readings by listing the books in the chronological order of their authors' lives. Doing this enables one to avoid any and all judgments about the scale of importance on which the books recommended might be arrayed.

Both alphabetical and chronological ordering exempt us from having to make value judgments. We are especially grateful for this if we fear, as many do, that making such judgments is likely to be tendentious or attributable to our purely personal prejudices.

There is still a further advantage to be gained by employing the alphabet or dates to arrange an assemblage of items. Not only are we exempt from having to make value judgments about the items being considered, but also we are free from the burden of having to think about what inner connections among them might suggest a significant pattern of their relationships to one another.

Alphabetization is particularly applicable to the items we find in reference books. But when it is also applied to the articles in a general encyclopedia or to the departments of learning in a university catalogue we are compelled to ask whether resorting solely to the alphabet is not an intellectual dereliction.

The immediate negative reply might be that an encyclopedia like a dictionary, or a university catalogue like a catalogue of library index cards, is after all just a reference tool—something to be used for look-it-up purposes only. A moment's reflection challenges that too-easy answer.

A great general encyclopedia is not just a reference book. It is also an instrument of learning in the same way that a great university is an institution of learning. Inherent in the things to be learned we should be able to find inner connections that might enable us to discover a significant pattern of their relationships to one another. We might even dare to construct a scale of values according to which we can judge their importance to us as things to be studied and learned. Instead of evading that challenge by saying nothing is more important to know than anything else, we should be willing to make judgments that scale the parts of knowledge from the less to the more important.

Not to do so where it is possible is an evasion of intellectual responsibility. Doing so does not necessitate abandoning an alphabetical ordering of the same materials for look-it-up or reference purposes. I would certainly not advocate a totally nonalphabetical encyclopedia, devoid of any use as a reference book; nor would I suggest that university catalogues be different from what they are now.

I am only saying that both need and deserve to be supplemented by an ordering that is more significant and intelligible than the one provided by alphabetization, which is no more significant or intelligible than a purely random array.

I have coined the word "alphabetiasis" to name the intellectual defect that consists in refusing to go beyond the alphabet where going beyond it is possible. It is strictly a modern malaise, more widespread in the twentieth century than at any earlier time.

Our universities invite us to embark on the sea of learning, but without charts and maps that might guide us in our progress or that might give us some significant direction in which to proceed. The same holds true, with a very few exceptions, of our great encyclopedias.

CHAPTER 2

Encyclopedias

SCHOLARS who write learned articles on the history of
encyclopedias tend to use that word in an extended sense.
This may puzzle contemporary readers who use it to refer to a set of books the contents of which are arranged
from A to Z. Paying attention to the meaning of the word's
Greek roots, scholars apply it to any collection of writings that provides a complete system of learning or an
all-around education. The collection of writings must
have, for its time and place, a scope that justifies regard-
ing it as encyclopedic in its dimensions.

The lectures of Aristotle delivered at his Lyceum in the
fourth century B.C., and later edited and compiled as an
orderly set of treatises, can be so regarded. Beginning with
treatises on physical phenomena and on the motion of
the heavens, followed by a large number of treatises
dealing with plants and animals and all the phenomena
of life, and completed by a treatise on the souls of living
organisms, the theoretical works of Aristotle reach their
culmination in a treatise to which his editors gave the
title "Metaphysics," the final sections of which are the-
ological. This series of works is then followed by treatises of another kind, practical rather than theoretical,
dealing with ethics, politics, rhetoric, and poetics. Pref-
acing the series as a whole are treatises on logic and the

method of the sciences, grouped together under the title "Organon."

Implicit in this ordering of Aristotle's works is a scheme for the organization of knowledge. As we shall subsequently discover when we return to it in another context, it represents the most comprehensive and most clearly articulated plan for the organization of knowledge that has come down to us from antiquity. But the whole corpus of Aristotle's works is not an encyclopedia in the modern sense of that term, nor was it intended to be one.

This is equally true of all the other examples that scholarly expositions of the history of encyclopedia point to in antiquity and the Middle Ages. *Natural History*, written by Pliny the Elder in the first century of our era, consists of thirty-seven books covering the arts as well as the sciences as then generally understood. Medieval compilations of all the knowledge then extant—one by Hugh of St. Victor and one by Vincent of Beauvais in the eleventh and twelfth centuries—are of a similar character.

All of these, like the collected works of Aristotle, are *encyclopedic* in the comprehensiveness of their coverage of all the knowledge existing at the time, but none is *an encyclopedia* of the kind that made its first appearance in the West in the seventeenth century. Nor are the elaborate collections of writings that the Chinese look back upon with pride and now call encyclopedias. They are anthologies of revered classics rather than systematic expositions of existing knowledge.

The first set of books constructed as a survey of existing knowledge appeared at the beginning of the eighteenth century, in 1704. It was the work of John Harris and was called by him a lexicon—*A Universal English Dictionary of the Arts and Sciences*. The use of the word "dictionary" in the subtitle notified readers that they could expect an alphabetical arrangement of the articles composing the work as a whole.

Harris's work was soon followed in the eighteenth century by that of Ephraim Chambers, who produced a two-volume work entitled *Cyclopedia; or an Universal Dictionary of the Arts and Sciences* (1728); by the famous French *Encyclopédie,* compiled by Diderot, d'Alembert, and their colleagues, issued in a series of volumes that began in 1751 and ended in 1778, twenty-eight volumes in all; and by the *Encyclopaedia Britannica,* published in Scotland in three volumes in the years 1768–1771. It, too, was called by its editors *A Dictionary of the Arts and Sciences,* the word "dictionary" being used in all these instances to signify the alphabetical arrangement of the articles that constituted the single comprehensive work.

The nineteenth century witnessed the proliferation of similar compilations constructed like lexicons or dictionaries—beginning with one by Brockhaus in Germany (1808), which inspired similar works in Danish, Swedish, Dutch, Russian, French, and Italian, and which were followed by an American effort, the *Encyclopedia Americana,* published in Philadelphia in thirteen volumes in the years 1829–1833. All of these comprised a large number of short popular articles on a wide variety of subjects that aimed at a comprehensiveness of coverage that deserved the name "encyclopedia."

The *Encyclopaedia Britannica* is distinguished from all the rest by the continuous history of its publication from 1768 to the present day in fifteen successive editions, growing from the three-volume first edition to the thirty-two volume fifteenth edition, currently in print. It is also distinguished by the arrangement of the articles that constituted its first edition.

In the first edition of *Encyclopaedia Britannica,* the

single alphabetical order of the articles was broken up into two quite different kinds of entries, all alphabetically arranged from A to Z.

On the one hand, there was a large number of extremely brief entries never more than a short paragraph and often consisting of a couple of lines, such as the entry on Japan, which is described as "a small island off the coast of California."

On the other hand, there was a relatively small number of extremely long articles—essays, dissertations, or treatises on the major subjects that expounded the knowledge the editors thought their readers should have about all the arts and sciences then recognized as having theoretical significance or practical importance.

Although these two types of entries were arranged in a single alphabetical sequence, they were distinguished typographically: the short entries resembling the entries in a lexicon of words with their definitions, and the long articles resembling books with many subdivisions, just as a book is divided into many chapters.

What follows is an enumeration by title of the major treatises or essays that appeared in the first edition of *Britannica*. It has interest for us as a representation of what the world of learning looked like in the eighteenth century. The alphabetical arrangement of these major articles in the first edition also clearly exemplifies the absence of any significant principle for the ordering of the parts of knowledge. As compared with Aristotle's non-alphabetical encyclopedic coverage of all the knowledge then extant, *Britannica's* alphabetical encyclopedia does not present us with anything like a systematic and principled organization of human knowledge.

Agriculture	Alligation	Annuities
Algebra	Anatomy	Architecture

Arithmetick	Geography	Musick
Astronomy	Grammar	
		Natural History
Bleaching	Horsemanship;	Navigation
Book-keeping	Or, The Art of Riding,	
Botany	and of Training and	Optics
Brewing	Managing Horses	
	Hydrostatics	Perspective
Chemistry		Pneumatics
Commerce	Law	
Conic Sections	Logic	Religion, or Theology
Electricity	Mechanics	Short-Hand Writing
	Medicine	Surgery
Farriery	Metaphysics	
Fluxions	Midwifery	Tanning
Fortification	Moral Philosophy,	Trigonometry
Gardening	or Morals	Watch and Clock Work

As far as I know, the first critic of the alphabetical arrangement of the articles in an encyclopedia was Samuel Taylor Coleridge at the beginning of the nineteenth century. He wrote a *Preliminary Treatise on Method* in which he set forth the principles for constructing an encyclopedia that was a systematic organization of knowledge rather than a mere alphabetical arrangement of articles, whether long or short. The *Encyclopedia Metropolitana*, which was to be that encyclopedia, he began but never finished.

We have in Coleridge's own words what he thought of all encyclopedias that, unlike the one he contemplated producing, suffered the defect of alphabetiasis. He wrote:

To call a huge unconnected miscellany of the *omne scibile* [the whole of knowledge], in any arrangement determined by the accident of initial letters, an encyclopedia, is the impudent ignorance of your Presbyterian bookmakers!

The Presbyterian bookmakers Coleridge had in mind must have been the Scottish editors of *Encyclopaedia Britannica*'s first edition. What he attributed to impudent ignorance might have been more generously explained as an effort on their part to make their encyclopedia useful as a reference book, in the same way that a dictionary is useful. A systematic, nonalphabetical order of articles may provide the users of an encyclopedia with an organization of knowledge—a map or chart of the world of learning—but it also prevents them from using it as a reference work in which they can easily look up something in which they are interested.

This conflict between two ways of constructing an encyclopedia, each with its merits and demerits, was not explicitly addressed in the continuous history of *Encyclopaedia Britannica* until the eleventh edition in the twentieth century, in 1911 to be precise. From the second to the great ninth edition, *Britannica* retained a single alphabetical arrangement without any effort to overcome its central defect—the absence of any indication of how the parts of knowledge are related to one another systematically.

When we come in this century to the eleventh edition, we find the following opening paragraphs in the Preface written by the editors.

It is not perhaps commonly realized that a general Encyclopaedia is more than a mere storehouse of facts. In reality it is also a systematic survey of all departments of knowledge.

But the alphabetical system of arrangement, with its obvious advantages, necessarily results in the separation from one another of articles dealing with any particular subject. Consequently the student who desires to make a complete study of a given topic must exercise his imagination if he seeks to exhaust the articles in which the topic is treated. Though the Index proper . . . will give him assistance in obtaining information under headings which are not themselves the titles of articles in the Encyclopaedia, he will still find it of the greatest service to have a bird's-eye view of all the articles upon his subject.

The ensuing pages of this volume contain what we believe to be the first attempt in any general work of reference at a systematic subject catalogue or analysis of the material contained in it.

What follows is an enumeration of the twenty-four general headings or main categories in the Classified Table of Contents under which are listed the more specific subjects treated in the encyclopedia.

I. Anthropology and Ethnology
II. Archaeology and Antiquities
III. Art
IV. Astronomy
V. Biology
VI. Chemistry
VII. Economics and Social Science
VIII. Education
IX. Engineering
X. Geography
XI. Geology
XII. History
XIII. Industries, Manufactures, and Occupations
XIV. Language and Writing
XV. Law and Political Science
XVI. Literature
XVII. Mathematics
XVIII. Medical Science
XIX. Military and Naval
XX. Philosophy and Psychology
XXI. Physics
XXII. Religion and Theology
XXIII. Sports and Pastimes
XXIV. Miscellaneous

Encyclopedias

Remarkable as it was at the time, this Classified Table of Contents did not succeed in overcoming the defects of an alphabetical arrangement of articles. It was not a systematic or topical organization of knowledge. An inspection of the foregoing list of twenty-four headings or categories immediately reveals that the alphabet was still the only thread on which the constituent parts of knowledge were strung.

Furthermore, under each of the alphabetically arranged main categories or general headings, from Anthropology to Religion and Theology (omitting Sports and Pastimes and Miscellaneous), the further subdivisions, after an initial enumeration of general subjects, consist of more specific headings, also alphabetically arranged.

For example, under the general heading Art, we find Architecture, Music, Painting and Engraving, Sculpture, Stage and Dancing, interrupted here and there by the heading Minor Arts. Beyond that, if we look at the listing of particular articles in this Classified Table of Contents, we find that their enumeration is also alphabetical.

What the editors of the eleventh edition said in their preface was unquestionably sound. A general encyclopedia should be "more than a mere storehouse of facts"—more than a reference book with alphabetically arranged entries that, like a dictionary, enables users to look something up. To do more than that, it must offer its users a mode of access to its contents other than the alphabet. It must, in one way or another, present its readers with a systematic or topical outline of knowledge that maps or charts the whole world of learning in a way that provides guidelines for the exploration of all its related parts.

With two or three notable exceptions, no encyclopedia so far completed in the twentieth century corrects the defects of alphabetiasis—a malady peculiar to modern times, and especially prevalent in our day. I will deal with these exceptions in Part Three after I review, in Part Two, ancient, medieval, and modern attempts to map or chart the world of learning, quite apart from the publication of encyclopedias constructed on the dictionary model.

But first let us continue the examination of the alphabetiasis that prevails today by turning from general encyclopedias to the catalogues of our great universities.

CHAPTER 3

Universities

AS we have seen, most encyclopedias, past and present, do not provide guidance for exploring the world of learning that they comprehensively cover. Nor do university catalogues. They, too, are mostly A to Z affairs. They cover everything, but in the range of subjects they present, one thing is not shown to be more important than another. A university catalogue is no more a guidebook to learning than a Sears Roebuck catalogue is a guidebook to buying.

Was this always the case? Or is it largely a twentieth-century phenomenon, symptomatic of the contemporary retreat from any effort to evaluate subjects and grade them on a scale of importance or significance?

When universities came into being in the twelfth and thirteenth centuries, in Padua and Paris, in Oxford and Cambridge, the main divisions of learning were manifest in the four faculties that constituted them. One of these was the faculty of arts. The other three were the professional faculties of medicine, law, and theology.

The latter, in the order named, corresponded to practical concerns of less and greater importance: the care of the body, the conduct of life and of society, and the salvation of the soul. In referring to these three areas of concern as practical, I am calling attention to the fact that the men who became doctors of medicine, of law, and of theology were not only men of learning, but also the *practitioners* of learned professions.

In contrast, the faculty of arts represented general as opposed to specialized learning, and learning for its own sake rather than for its useful application to some special field of practice or action. This faculty consisted of teachers who bore the title Master of Arts. The students they succeeded in initiating into the world of general learning were certified as Bachelors of Arts.

As it is generally used today to signify mainly the fine arts, and sometimes even more narrowly the visual arts as differentiated from literature, music, and other fine arts, the word "arts" does not convey the scope of this non-professional branch of a medieval university. What was signified by the word "arts" included *all* the liberal arts, both those of language and those of mathematics. It also included all the sciences, which were regarded as branches of philosophy, both speculative or theoretical and practical or moral.

The faculty of arts might, therefore, have been more appropriately called the philosophical faculty or even, perhaps, the faculty of the humanities or of humane letters. But once again we must guard against the current use of these terms by remembering that the Latin word "humanitas," translating the Greek word "paideia," signifies general as opposed to specialized learning. Thus understood, it includes all branches of learning, not just those that remain after we have named the various sciences, natural and social. We must also remember that philosophy once meant the kind of learning that was everybody's business, not—as it has become in our day—a highly technical field of specialized scholarship.

It was not until the nineteenth century that German

universities introduced the degree of doctor of philosophy to go along with the three professional doctorates in medicine, law, and theology. When that happened philosophy no longer stood for general as opposed to specialized learning. On the contrary, the faculty of philosophy comprehended within its scope all branches of specialized scholarship, as specialized as medicine, law, and theology, but differentiated from them by virtue of the fact that these branches of specialized scholarship were devoted to the advancement of learning for its own sake, not for the sake of applying knowledge in practice or action.

As originally established in the German universities of the last century, the Ph.D. degree signified competence in research and was awarded to scholars who intended to devote themselves mainly to research. It was not a degree that was also supposed to certify competence in teaching, as it has become in American universities today.

That the doctorate of philosophy was in origin, and still persists as, a mark of specialized scholarship rather than of broad, general, or humanistic learning is plainly indicated by the qualification that the degree always carries. One never receives a doctorate in philosophy *as such*, but instead a Ph.D. in history, or in English, physics, geology, economics, and so on. Even when one receives a Ph.D. in philosophy, it is not in philosophy as a general comprehension of all the arts and sciences, but in philosophy as just one among the many specialized fields of study offered in a modern university.

The oldest academic organization in the United States, concerned with the advancement of knowledge but not with the dissemination of it by teaching, is the American Philosophical Society. It was founded by Benjamin Franklin in 1743; by 1769 it had established six areas of research, as follows: Geography, Mathematics, Natural Philosophy, and Astronomy; Medicine and Anatomy; Natural History and Chemistry; Trade and Commerce; Mechanics and Architecture; and Husbandry and American Improvements. The year 1815 brought with it the addition of a seventh area: History, Moral Science, and General Literature.

The foregoing was simplified in 1936 by a regrouping of these areas under four headings: Mathematics and Physical Sciences; Geological and Biological Sciences; Social Sciences; and Humanities.

Many American universities today have adopted something like this fourfold classification of all departments of research and instruction. Sometimes it is a threefold classification, as in Columbia University's Graduate School of Arts and Sciences, which is partitioned into the Social Sciences, the Natural Sciences, and the Humanities. In any case, what is now called Humanities is the residue that remains after all the branches of science have been listed.

The listing is, as might be expected, mostly alphabetical. Thus, under Columbia's general heading of Natural Sciences, we find:

Anatomy and Cell Biology

Applied Physics and
  Nuclear Engineering

Astronomy

Biochemistry

Biological Sciences

Chemical Engineering and
  Applied Chemistry

Chemistry

Civil Engineering and
  Engineering Mechanics

Computer Science

Electrical Engineering

Geological Sciences

Human Genetics and
  Development

Industrial Engineering and
  Operations Research

Mathematics

Mechanical Engineering

Microbiology

Mining, Metallurgical, and
   Mineral Engineering
Pathology
Pharmacology

Physics
Physiology
Psychology
Statistics

Under Social Sciences, we find:

Anthropology
Economics
Geography

History
Political Science
Sociology

And under Humanities, the following:

Art History and
   Archaeology
Classics
East Asian Languages and
   Cultures
English and Comparative
   Literature
French and Romance
   Philology
Germanic Languages

Italian
Linguistics
Middle East Languages and
   Cultures
Music
Philosophy
Religion
Slavic Languages
Spanish and Portuguese

Whether under a fourfold or a threefold division, the number of departments in our university graduate schools is constantly on the increase. At Harvard University in 1919, there were fifteen academic departments. This increased to twenty-eight in 1949 and to thirty-one in 1976. At Princeton University, the number of departments increased from fourteen in 1919 to twenty-six in 1976; at the University of California at Berkeley, from thirty-nine in 1919 to forty-three in 1976.

These increases are largely due to the proliferation of the specialized sciences. When it was set up in 1863, the

National Academy of Sciences comprised ten sections. In a major reorganization that took place in 1975, this increased to twenty-three sections, the additions consisting entirely of sciences that did not exist one hundred years ago.

The same proliferation has occurred in the professional schools of our universities. In addition to the three learned professions of medicine, law, and theology that have come down to us from the Middle Ages, we now have schools of business, of journalism, of social service, of dentistry, of nursing, of engineering (with all its various subdivisions), of computer technology, of education, of library science, of architecture, of agriculture, of animal husbandry, and so on. The foregoing enumeration, although not alphabetical, is as much a random order as an alphabetical listing would be.

If we turn from our university's graduate and professional schools to their undergraduate colleges, the alphabetical arrangement of courses in the catalogue is determined by the initial letter in the name of the academic department under the auspices of which these course of instruction are given.

The alphabetical lists of departments in our colleges are much too long to be reproduced here in full. To serve the same purpose, I think it will suffice to present comparable samplings from four such lists, taken from the current catalogues of Columbia University, Yale University, Harvard University, and the University of California at Berkeley.

In each case, the comparable samples consist of departments running from C through F. These relatively short samples will enable the reader to compare them at a glance and to note how they differ, either by what they add or what they omit. The differences represent a concern with subjects deemed of some importance for undergraduate instruction. But in all four cases, readers should also note that all the departments named appear to have equal status, one no more important in the realm of learning than another. These four alphabetical displays can be taken as fairly representative of what is offered in almost all of our major colleges and universities. Here and there, as in Columbia's two requirements and in Harvard's six-pronged

COLUMBIA	YALE
Chemistry	Cell Biology
Classics	Chemistry
Computer Science	Classical Languages and Lit-
Contemporary Civilization	·eratures
Dance	Comparative Literature
East Asian Languages and	Computer Science
Cultures	East Asian Languages and
Economics	Literatures
Education	East Asian Studies
Engineering	Economic History
English and Comparative	Economics
Literature	Engineering and Applied
Film	Science
French Language and Liter-	English
ature	Epidemiology and Public
	Health
	Experimental Pathology
	Forestry and Environmental
	Studies
	French

HARVARD	UNIVERSITY OF CALIFORNIA
Celtic Languages and Literatures	Chemistry
Chemical Physics	Chicano Studies
Chemistry	Classics
The Classics	Comparative Literature
Comparative Literature	Computer Science
Computer Science	Development Studies
Dramatic Arts	Dramatic Arts
Earth and Planetary Physics	Dutch Studies
East Asian Languages and Civilizations	East European Studies
East Asian Programs	Economics
Economics	English
Engineering Sciences and Applied Physics	Environmental Sciences
English and American Literature and Language	Ethnic Studies
European Studies	Film
Expository Writing	Folklore
Fine Arts	French
Folklore and Mythology	
French Language and Literature	

core requirement, certain fields of study are singled out as indispensable for the acquisition of general learning. These are among the few exceptions to the unrelieved alphabetiasis of college offerings.

Beyond such requirements where they exist, students

can exercise freedom of choice with regard to the subjects that will be of major or minor interest to them. The alphabetical listing of courses gives them no guidance at all for the exercise of that choice. It does not tell them which subjects should be of major and which of minor interest to them, and why. It leaves their choice of majors and minors to the vagaries of their own ill-informed current interests.

CHAPTER 4

Libraries

IT has been said that it is the mission of the wise man, or of his less than *alter ego*, the philosopher, to judge the value of things and to order them according to their merit. Resorting to the alphabet as an organizing principle avoids making the judgments antecedent to an ordering that reflects relative worth, importance, or significance. It is an abdication of wisdom and philosophy, all for the sake of convenient reference.

In the chapters of Part Two, we shall consider how philosophers—ancient, medieval, and modern—have performed their ministry in the name of wisdom. But before we come to that, we must look at one more unphilosophical approach to the problem of structuring the whole world of learning, putting its parts in significant relation to one another.

The approach I have in mind is that of librarians engaged in the task of classifying the books they must put on their shelves in some orderly way. Alphabetizing them by reference to the initial letter of the author's name would certainly not do; nor would it be useful to arrange them chronologically by date of publication. Such an alphabetical or chronological organization sometimes occurs in cataloguing the books in a library, but not in a system of classification.

Encyclopedias, universities, and libraries have a certain similarity. All three, when they attain a certain magnitude, claim to be covering the whole sphere of what is known, the whole realm of human learning at a given time. A great encyclopedia covers it by articles that survey and expound the parts and parcels of that whole, a great university by the courses it offers, and a great library by the books it puts on its shelves.

This parallelism might suggest that all three would organize those parts and parcels in the same way. As we have seen, this is true of encyclopedias and catalogues of university courses. Both employ the alphabet, but libraries do not.

We do not know in what order the manuscript papyri were laid out in the great library of Alexandria that was burned to the ground by the Romans when they invaded Egypt in the first century B.C. But it would be reasonable to suppose that it was probably in accordance with Aristotelian principles. The same might be said of the great libraries of Salamanca and Toledo in Moorish Spain in the Middle Ages. Here, too, the ordering principles would probably have been derived from the Islamic philosophers Avicenna and Averroës, both followers of Aristotle.

When we come to libraries that, after Gutenberg, first put printed books on shelves, it would again be reasonable to expect that the ordering principles adopted by libraries would follow the scheme for the organization of knowledge to be found in Francis Bacon's *Advancement of Learning*. In the modern world, certainly in its early centuries, Bacon replaced Aristotle as the organizer of knowledge.

Bacon's scheme in brief (we shall deal with it at greater length later) was based on a threefold division of the human faculties at work in the products of the mind, certainly in the production of books. Named in an ascending order, they are memory, imagination, and reason. History and biography, for example, belong in the sphere of memory; poetry and fiction belong in the sphere of the imagination; and all the sciences, or parts of philosophy, belong in the sphere of reason.

When Thomas Jefferson built a library for himself at his home in Monticello, Virginia, and shelved his own collection of books there, he put them in an order that corresponded to Bacon's scheme. Jefferson's library later became the nucleus of the Library of Congress. The threefold division of books proposed by Bacon necessarily required a great many subdivisions in order to accommodate the immense variety of books that fell under each of the main categories. With forty-four subdivisions added, the classification scheme of the Library of Congress remained unchanged from Jefferson's time until the beginning of the twentieth century, when it was completely revised. That undertaking, begun in 1901, was completed in 1910.

Here is the Library of Congress's cataloguing plan as it stands today. I have omitted the category of reference books (encyclopedias, dictionaries, etc.), that heads the list. Under some of the main categories I have indicated examples of what are included as subordinate classes of works.

Philosophy

Psychology

Religion

History, including Biography

Geography, including Travel and Physical Geography Anthropology, and Folklore

Social sciences, including Statistics

Economics
Transportation and
    Communication
Commerce
Finance
Sociology
Associations, Societies
Socialism, Communism
Social pathology,
    Criminology,
    Penology
Political science, Con-
    stitutional history,
    Administration, and
    International law
Law
Education

Music

Fine arts, including
    Architecture

Language and Literature

Science, including
    Mathematics
    Physics
    Chemistry
    Biological sciences

Medicine

Agriculture

Technology, including
    Engineering
    Building
    Chemical technology
    Manufactures

Military science, Naval
    science

Bibliography and Library
    science

Under the main category of Fine Arts, the order of the subdivisions is as follows: visual arts, architecture, sculpture, drawing, design, illustration, painting. Under the main category of Science, the order of the subdivisions is as follows: mathematics, mathematical logic, computer science, astronomy, physics, chemistry, geology, natural history, general biology, cytology, botany, zoology, human anatomy, physiology, microbiology. And subordinate to the main categories of Philosophy, Psychology, and Religion are: logic, speculative philosophy, metaphysics, epistemology, methodology, aesthetics, ethics, mythology, and the names of various world religions.

One comment made about the Library of Congress's classification scheme has said of it that "it does not pretend to be philosophically sound; it merely seeks to be pragmatic." That is an understatement. Nothing could be more unsound philosophically, by reference to either Aristotelian or Baconian principles. Jefferson's nuclear library may have started out to be Baconian in organization, but the twentieth-century revision of the original plan departed from it in a variety of different directions.

The other major scheme for organizing libraries is that first put into effect in 1873 by Melvil Dewey when he was the librarian of Amherst College. This became in the twentieth century the Dewey Decimal System. In its original form it comprised nine major classes or categories, which Dewey thought he had placed in a descending order that was simply the inverse of Bacon's ascending order from history (memory), through poetic literature and fiction (imagination) to science and philosophy (reason).

How far that is from being the case can be seen at once by looking at the order in which the main categories of the Dewey Decimal System are placed.

Bibliography and Library
  science

Philosophy

Psychology

Religion

Social sciences, including
  Sociology
  Statistics
  Political science
  Economics
  Law

Public administration
Welfare and
  Associations
Education
Commerce
Customs and Folklore

Language

Science, including
  Mathematics
  Physics
  Chemistry
  Biological sciences

Medicine	Fine arts, including
Technology, including	Architecture and Music
Engineering	Literature
Agriculture	Geography
Business	
Chemical technology	Biography
Manufactures	History
Building	

Both the Library of Congress scheme and the Dewey Decimal System raise a host of philosophical questions that remain unanswered. To what extent are the main categories coordinate, or on the same level, with one another, and to what extent is there a hierarchical ordering of things that are supraordinate and subordinate to one another? If there is a hierarchical ordering, are the gradations of importance in an ascending or a descending scale? Are the subdivisions of some of the main categories appropriately named?

For example, should mathematics and logic be placed in the company of the empirical or experimental sciences? Should religion be closely associated with philosophy? Does psychology belong with philosophy or with the experimental sciences? Are there two quite different disciplines that can be called psychology, one that is a branch of philosophy and one that is an empirical science? And does the latter belong with the natural sciences or with the social sciences?

Such questions are plainly and completely avoided by recourse to the alphabet in encyclopedias and in university catalogues. But when the bibliographical systems of great libraries place their main categories in a nonalphabetical order, it is impossible to avoid raising such questions. Once the alphabet is abandoned, other principles must be employed, and they are subject to being challenged for their soundness and adequacy.

We must turn to the philosophers for answers to the kinds of questions raised by our consideration of the unphilosophical systems currently used by the great libraries of the world. Answers there are aplenty, differing from epoch to epoch, as we will see in the chapters of Part Two that follow. If we cannot adopt any of them without reservations or qualifications, we may at least be able to draw from them insights and inspirations that will serve as guidelines for anyone's exploration of the world of learning.

PART TWO

THE ORGANIZATION OF KNOWLEDGE PRIOR TO THE TWENTIETH CENTURY

It is necessary to call into council the views of our predecessors in order that we may profit by whatever is sound in their views and avoid their errors.

ARISTOTLE: *On the Soul,*
Book I, Chapter 2

CHAPTER 5

Greek and Roman Antiquity

Plato (428–384 B.C.)

UNLIKE many of the schemes for the organization of knowledge that we shall come to later, the plan that Plato gives us is pedagogical. The subjects to be studied are arranged in the order in which they should be learned, an order that corresponds to successive stages in the development of the individual from childhood and youth to the full maturity of life's ripest years.

The context in which Plato outlines his regimen for a life of learning occurs in those books of the *Republic* in which he lays down his plan for the education of the guardians of the ideal state—its ruling class. It is not an organization of the parts of knowledge as such, in which different kinds of knowledge are related according to differences in their objects or subject matter. That may be implicit in it, but explicitly it is a temporal succession, placing first what should come first in the development of the mind and then, through intermediate stages, coming last to what should be the crowning culmination of the mind's journey on the road to wisdom and truth. It can, therefore, be regarded as a road map for the guidance of a lifetime of learning.

The terms Plato uses may not convey to the contemporary reader the elements of his plan as they would be understood today. I shall, therefore, translate his vocabulary into the more familiar terminology of our own day.

The period of childhood and youth, Plato thinks, should be devoted to gymnastics and music—gymnastics conferring upon the body the strength and skills that render it serviceable, and music being the cultivation of the sensibilities, the memory, and the imagination. During the later years of this first phase, gymnastics and music are to be supplemented by the acquisition of skill in the use of language, together with skill in the employment of the mind in the processes of definition, analysis, reasoning, and argument.

We cannot help being surprised by the fact that Plato assigns the first twenty years of life to this first phase of learning. But we must remember that this program is intended for the guardian or ruling class, persons with ample free time, not for those who will engage much earlier in all forms of productive labor.

The second phase, occurring in the years between twenty and thirty, turns the mind away from the world of the senses and toward the intelligible realm that is constituted by the objects of mathematical thought and the demonstrations of mathematical science—the realm of numbers and figures, of ratios and proportions.

Plato's names for these elements in his order of learning are arithmetic, geometry, astronomy, and music. Of these, the first two are familiar terms for us. But for Plato, astronomy and music in this second phase are also mathematical sciences, the one dealing with the mathematical formulation of the celestial motions, the other with the ratios and proportions of harmonics.

Between the ages of thirty and fifty, the guardians slowly achieve full maturity through engagement in the affairs of state. This is a period devoted to profiting from experience in human affairs rather than one that involves the study of this or that subject matter. Their minds *3rd* have been disciplined and cultivated by the subjects studied in the first two phases, and having been matured and enriched by the experiences acquired in the third phase, the guardians are now prepared for the fourth and final phase.

It is here that the development of their minds attains its highest elevation, their pursuit of truth reaches its culmination, and their search for wisdom approaches its *4th* goal. This is the phase that Plato devotes to dialectic, his name for philosophy in its purest form—the contemplation of ideas and the grasp of first principles. Here at last the mind has turned completely away from the world of sensible and changing things, the realm of becoming, and concentrates entirely on the realm of intelligible and immutable being.

One part or area of knowledge to which we today give a major share of our attention is almost totally absent from the Platonic scheme. Readers will have noticed that there is no mention of the natural sciences, sciences that involve observation of sensible phenomena. The one Platonic dialogue that deals with the formation and development of the cosmos, the *Timaeus*, includes a comment by Socrates to the effect that this cosmological exposition is only a "likely story," more like a myth than a scientific demonstration.

If readers also wonder where in Plato's scheme the good life and the good society become matters to be thought about and studied, they must be told that ethics and politics are not, for Plato, sciences that occupy a place in the organization of knowledge. Such matters are to be thought about in the study of ideas—the idea of the good, of happiness and virtue, of the state and justice.

One further point remains. In many of his earlier dia-

logues, such as *The Gorgias,* and in one of his later dia-
logues, *The Sophist,* Plato is concerned to differentiate
the dialectician from the rhetorician and the sophist. All
three employ the same, or very similar, methods. All three
are skilled in the same or very similar uses of the mind.
But the essential and crucial difference for Plato is that
the dialectician's intellectual processes are governed
throughout by dedication to the truth, whereas both the
rhetorician and the sophist, often the same person, aim
only to win the argument, regardless of the truth about
the matters under consideration.

Aristotle (384–322 B.C.)

Aristotle's organization of knowledge resembles Plato's educational plan in three respects.

First, like Plato, Aristotle places at the outset of learning the disciplines governing the use of language and the
operations of the mind, skills conferred by the study of
grammar and logic. The initial work in the corpus of
Aristotelian writings is called the *Organon,* which consists of a series of treatises that deal with the use of words,
the interpretation and analysis of statements, the rules of
reasoning, the methods of science, and the devices of ar-
gumentation. Competence in such matters is preparatory
for all further learning. That is why it precedes all
the rest.

The second point of similarity lies in the fact that
Aristotle, like Plato, reserves the study of certain subjects for that period of life when, through the dint of much
experience, individuals have attained full maturity. He
tells us that the study of ethics and politics is not for the
young. They do not have enough experience of human
affairs to make sound judgments about what ought to be

sought and ought to be done in the conduct of life and in the government of society.

The third respect in which Plato and Aristotle appear to be of one mind, although the terms they use are quite different, has to do with the culmination or highest level of study in the pursuit of theoretical truth and of philosophical wisdom. This, as we have seen, goes by the name of dialectic for Plato and is the study of ideas; whereas, for Aristotle, this is the highest of all sciences, sometimes called metaphysics, sometimes the first philosophy, and sometimes theology.

Each of the three names is appropriate: "metaphysics," inasmuch as the science in question goes beyond physics and is concerned with being rather than change, motion, or becoming; "first philosophy," because it deals with first principles, principles underlying and common to all other branches of knowledge; and "theology," because its concluding chapters are concerned with God.

With these similarities acknowledged, we find many significant differences. One is that Aristotle puts into his scheme a whole set of sciences that Plato omits; namely, the sciences that give us knowledge of the physical world and of the observable phenomena of nature. In the collection of Aristotelian writings, the grammatical and logical treatises of the *Organon* are directly followed by physical treatises that deal with terrestrial change, motion, generation, and corruption, with the causes operative in all these transformations, and with space, time, and eternity. These are followed by a treatise that deals with celestial motions. Next in line come a whole series of biological works, sciences concerned with the classification of plants and animals, with their procreation or generation, and with their parts or vital organs.

The last in this series of works is a treatise on the soul—

Aristotle's psychology. It deals with the scale of living things and with the vegetative powers of plant organisms and the sensitive and locomotive powers of animal organisms before coming to the sensitive and intellectual powers of human organisms. In this latter connection, Aristotle's psychology serves as a bridge from his physical and biological sciences to his purely philosophical work, his *Metaphysics*.

It is necessary to remember that in Aristotle's day the words "science" and "philosophy" did not have the connotations they have today, which signify two quite different kinds of inquiry and types of knowledge. Nevertheless, it is sufficiently clear that, with the exception of the treatise called *Physics*, which is more natural philosophy than natural science, the rest, especially Aristotle's biological treatises, are empirical and investigative sciences based on the observation of natural phenomena. They represent the beginnings of empirical science in the modern sense of that term.

In sharp contrast, Aristotle's *Physics* and *Metaphysics* are philosophical works that do not involve empirical investigation, even though their reflective and analytical thought is based to a certain extent on simple, common experiences that all of us enjoy without our making any deliberate effort to investigate.

In order to differentiate metaphysics from, and relate it to, other sciences, Aristotle established a hierarchy of the theoretical branches of knowledge. In this ascending scale, the lowest rung is occupied by the natural sciences, dealing with sensible, changing things. A gradation higher is mathematics, being the study of abstract or ideal objects. Numbers and figures exist as objects of thought, whether or not they also have any mode of existence in physical reality. Metaphysics stands at the highest level, above mathematics. It is like mathematics in that it deals with purely intelligible objects, but it goes beyond mathematics in reaching to objects of thought that can also have real existence apart from the world of sensible, material things.

A second major differentiating feature of Aristotle's organization of knowledge lies in his sharp distinction between knowledge that is theoretical and to be studied for its own sake and knowledge that is practical and to be studied for the sake of actions to be prescribed, regulated, and judged. Physics, mathematics, and metaphysics constitute the three grades of theoretical knowledge; ethics, economics, and politics, the three kinds of practical science. They can be grouped together under the general heading of moral philosophy.

There is still a third division in the classification of the parts of knowledge that we find in Aristotle's scheme but not in Plato's. To the theoretical and practical sciences, Aristotle adds the study of the productive arts, both the fine and the useful arts, the former productive of things to be enjoyed for their beauty, the latter productive of things to be of service in achieving some desired result. Aristotle's treatment of the fine arts, in a book entitled *Poetics*, is mainly concerned with epic and dramatic literature. His treatment of the useful arts occurs in those scientific treatises in which he compares the productions of art with the productions of nature.

Readers will have observed the absence, from both the Platonic and the Aristotelian schemes, of certain parts of knowledge that are given prominence in any modern enumeration of subjects that deserve consideration. History is not mentioned at all by Plato. It is mentioned by Aristotle in a single passage in which he says that poetry is more philosophical than history because it has a certain measure of universality. Poetry portrays actions that are possible and even probable, while history must confine itself to the narration of what has actually happened and is therefore limited to particulars.

Other disciplines of modern origin and contemporary importance do not appear, such as sociology or anthropology in the field of the behavioral sciences, or chemistry in the field of the physical sciences. While theology has a position of high esteem for both Plato and Aristotle, neither devote much, if any, attention to religion.

The Roman Stoics
(First and Second Centuries A.D.)

The Roman Stoics present us with a tripartite division of knowledge that has an attractive simplicity and a common touch. According to them, the three parts of human knowledge are logic, physics, and ethics—the study of the principles and laws of human thought, the study of the principles and laws of nature, the study of the principles and rules of human conduct.

As far as I can tell, none of the leading Stoic philosophers assigned priority or superiority to one of these three parts as compared with the others. Nevertheless one might, as a matter of common sense, regard the study of logic as preparatory to the other two kinds of knowledge.

Stoic philosophy placed great emphasis on the station that man occupies in the natural scheme of things. In conformity with that view, one would make physics precede ethics, as logic precedes them both. The study of the laws of nature throws light on what is right and good in the sphere of human conduct. To be of good will is to act in accordance with the laws of nature.

Augustine (354–430)

St. Augustine, being a Christian theologian as well as a Roman philosopher, alters the picture of the realm of learning that he inherited from his Greek predecessors. For him, it is not speculative theology as a branch of philosophy that stands at the apex of human knowledge, but rather the knowledge possessed by those who have religious faith in the revealed word of God.

In other respects, Augustine is a Platonist who adds little to the teaching of Plato. Himself a student and teacher of rhetoric, he lays stress on that art along with the related arts of grammar and logic as indispensable instruments of learning, not just as tools of communication. He adopts Plato's conception of dialectic as the highest reach of philosophical thought, always, of course, with the qualification that above it lies the truth and the wisdom to be found by persons of religious faith in Sacred Scripture.

CHAPTER 6

The Middle Ages

Thomas Aquinas (1225–1274)

BOTH great Christian theologians, Aquinas and Augustine, differ in their discipleship—the former to Aristotle, the latter to Plato. They also differ in the times in which they lived—Aquinas at the high point of the Middle Ages, Augustine at the very end of ancient civilization with the fall of Rome to the barbarians from the north.

These differences account for the different views they take of the place of theology, or what Aquinas called Sacred Doctrine, in the organization of knowledge.

Both men place the knowledge that comes with faith at the summit of everything that can be known; both regard such knowledge as supernatural in origin, a gift from God through the revelation of Himself to mankind. All other knowledge is acquired through the exercise of man's natural faculties, his senses and his intellect. But for Augustine, the knowledge acquired through faith, not through reason, is superior to scientific knowledge, which proceeds from premises it adopts to the demonstration of conclusions.

Aquinas, on the contrary, regards Sacred Doctrine or sacred theology as the very epitome of science. It receives its principles or premises from the articles of Christian faith, dogmatically declared; and proceeds therefrom by rational processes to analyses, clarifications, and conclusions that provide the faithful with a better understanding of their religious beliefs. The rational processes whereby dogmatic or sacred theology is developed from the articles of faith call upon all the insights, distinctions, and arguments that philosophy can make available.

That is why Aquinas not only esteems theology as the queen of the sciences, but also praises philosophy as her indispensable handmaiden. In this conception of philosophy as theology's useful servant, philosophy encompasses more than metaphysics and ethics. It includes the sciences that comprise the range of natural knowledge.

Philosophy at its own twin summits in metaphysics and ethics confers upon mankind a modicum of theoretical and practical wisdom, but not enough for the Christian life, either in this world or for salvation in the next. Its deficiencies must be overcome by the superior wisdom that comes only with faith.

What kind of training and formation must be given the developing mind in order to prepare it to receive and embrace that superior wisdom? Where Augustine placed the study of grammar and rhetoric in the earliest stage of learning, Aquinas, as Master of Arts at the University of Paris in the thirteenth century, prepared his students for theology by reading to them from the philosophical works of Aristotle, and commenting on what he read, passage by passage.

For the students to follow his commentaries, they first had to be trained in what were then called the seven liberal arts. Although all seven had been recognized in one form or another by Plato and Aristotle, they were not formulated as a trivium and quadrivium of studies in

Augustine's day. That came about in the medieval schools and universities of a later day.

The trivium comprised the three arts of grammar, rhetoric, and logic—the arts of using language correctly and effectively and the arts of using one's mind with precision, accuracy, and cogency. Logic was not only an art—a skill and a method; it was also a science that had principles of its own, definitions, distinctions, and axioms that established a host of rules—the laws of thought. The same can be said of rhetoric and grammar. They, too, were sciences as well as arts.

The remaining four of the seven liberal arts—the arts of the quadrivium—would appear at first blush to be mainly science: arithmetic, geometry, astronomy (i.e., the mathematical science of the spheres), and music (i.e., the mathematical science of harmonics). But they, too, are arts, skills of the mind in operating with numbers and figures, ratios and proportions.

The seven liberal disciplines have their aspect as arts in the operational skills they confer upon the mind. They have their scientific aspect in the principles they appeal to and the rules or conclusions they establish. As arts, they provide us with intellectual know-how. As sciences, they give us knowledge about the intelligible objects that the mind contemplates when it reflects upon its own acts and its own conceptual abstractions.

Roger Bacon (1214–1292)

A contemporary of Thomas Aquinas, and an associate of his at the University of Paris, to which he had come from the University of Oxford, Roger Bacon was far more a natural scientist than either a theologian or a metaphysician. We would, therefore, naturally expect from him a quite different approach to the organization of knowledge and to the order of learning.

In his *Opus Majus*, Bacon stressed the utility of the mathematical sciences in their application to astronomy, optics, chronology, and other disciplines. We find what, at this early date, may seem surprising to us—a call for the establishment of experimental science as a method of investigation and verification in our effort to know the facts of nature. And, as we might expect from a Franciscan friar, we find an acknowledgment of a close affinity between philosophy and theology, and the elevation of moral philosophy and theology to the apex of human learning because it treats of man's relation to God.

In another of Bacon's works, of which we have only portions left, the four extant volumes indicate an ascending order of subjects to be studied. They are: *first*, the arts of the trivium—grammar, rhetoric, and logic; *second*, the arts of the quadrivium, beginning with the common principles of mathematics and going on to its special branches—arithmetic, geometry, astronomy, and music; *third*, the whole range of the natural sciences, including optics, geography, alchemy, agriculture, medicine, and experimental science in general; and *fourth*, metaphysics and morals as the crowning subjects to be studied.

CHAPTER 7

Modern Times:
Seventeenth Century

Francis Bacon (1561–1626)

FRANCIS Bacon—Baron Verulam, Keeper of the Privy Seal and Lord Chancellor of England—brought the talents of a judge and administrator to the philosophical problems he addressed. His personal physician, William Harvey, the discoverer of the circulation of the blood, said of him that he "wrote philosophy like a lord chancellor."

Of the two books that established Bacon's reputation and spread his influence—*The Advancement of Learning*, published in 1605, and the *Novum Organum*, published in 1620—only the first concerns us here. It is of interest to us but not for the reason Bacon wrote it.

Bacon's principal aim was to take stock of the state of human knowledge in his day and to point out the areas in which there were deficiencies, these to be remedied for the sake of increasing the general store of human learning. In order to do that he had first to schematize the whole field of knowledge, indicating its several parts and their relationship to one another. His map or chart of human learning, which he himself referred to as a "small globe of the intellectual world," had greater amplitude than those words imply. It was expansive and comprehensive.

The principle he employed in his organization of knowledge derived from the distinction of the human faculties—memory, imagination, and reason. From the exercise of these cognitive faculties all of the knowledge that man possesses by natural means is obtained. But man also has knowledge from another, a supernatural, source— divine revelation. Bacon did not treat the latter in any detail. Concerned with what needs to be done to advance human learning, his differentiation of the parts of knowledge fell principally within the first of these two spheres.

By reference to the three faculties of memory, imagination, and reason, Bacon distinguished history, poetry, and philosophy. History deals with the memorable past that has become a matter of record. Poetry for Bacon covers all the products of our imagination—the whole of imaginative literature, not just lyrics in verse, but all forms of narrative fiction, both dramatic and epic (which we now call plays and novels), whether written in prose or in verse.

As Bacon used the word "philosophy" it had a much broader connotation than it has today. It included all the forms of knowledge obtained by reason's reflections on human experience, aided in some instances by experimental investigation or inquiry. It took into account what we would call the sciences as well as what we would call the branches of philosophy. It also included the technological or productive results of experimental science and the various arts that involved other applications of science.

The fact, pointed out by Bacon's critics, that these three main parts of human knowledge do not stem exclusively from memory, imagination, and reason, does not, in my judgment, undermine his controlling insight. Of course, reason and imagination, as well as memory, enter into historical knowledge, both on the side of historical research and on the side of historical narration. But without the operation of memory, there would be no history. Similarly, memory and imagination enter into the philosophical or scientific enterprise in all its forms, but without the exercise of reason, there would be no philosophy or science. Reason and memory, too, play a part in the compositions of poetry, but without the play of imagination there would be no imaginative literature.

The point on which Bacon can be challenged and perhaps also corrected is the inclusion of poetry or imaginative literature as one of the three parts of human knowledge. That it is an essential component of human culture, and of learning in the broadest sense of that term, lies beyond question. But if knowledge is used in a narrower sense than learning, if it is used for what claims to be true of reality, where such claims are verifiable or falsifiable, then history and philosophy or science belong in the domain of knowledge, poetry does not.

On the other hand, it can be said that truth is more ample, that it includes poetic as well as scientific, philosophical, and historical truth. It includes truth about the possible as well as truth about the actual. On that basis, Bacon's inclusion of poetry along with history and philosophy in the domain of knowledge can be justified.

History, according to Bacon, has four subdivisions. The terms he used to name them need some explanation for contemporary readers. Under natural history, he included not only what we would mean by that term but also the histories of the arts and sciences. Under civil history, he included biographies and chronicles as well as the history of political institutions and affairs. Under ecclesiastical history, he included the history of the church and other religious institutions, practices, and events. Under literary history, he included what we would call social and cultural, as contrasted with narrowly political, history.

This classification of the subdivisions of history raises some questions. Does not natural history, in the sense in which that term is now used for an account of changes in the realm of the phenomena of nature, belong with the natural sciences rather than with political and cultural history? Should not ecclesiastical history, if it is strictly human and not divine knowledge (i.e., not based on Sacred Scriptures or divine revelation), be an element in cultural history? In any case, it is clear that what Bacon meant by ecclesiastical history was concerned only with the institutions and events of the Christian religion. Nothing could have been further from his mind than what we mean by the comparative study of all human religions.

Finally we come to philosophy, the third main division of human learning or knowledge. Here the primary subdivision separates the consideration of the most general principles of all knowledge from the conclusions of special forms of inquiry. This gives us, on the one hand, what Bacon called *philosophia prima*, which corresponds in part, but only in part, to what the ancients called metaphysics. The special disciplines or modes of inquiry are then further subdivided according to the objects with which they are concerned—God, nature, and man. Thus we get a threefold subdivision of the special disciplines into 1) natural, as distinguished from sacred, theology; 2) natural philosophy; and 3) human philosophy.

Once again, it is necessary to translate Bacon's nomenclature into terms more familiar and recognizable to the contemporary world. What Bacon called natural theology, we would refer to as philosophical theology. For the ancients, this would have constituted the concluding chapters of a treatise on metaphysics. What Bacon called natural philosophy, we would separate into the philosophy of nature on the one hand, and all the natural sciences on the other. What Bacon called human philosophy, he subdivided into one part that dealt with human beings as individuals, and another part that dealt with human beings in aggregate or in association—with human society.

In the part concerned with human individuals, Bacon separated the disciplines concerned with the human body, such as medicine, cosmetics, and cooking, from the disciplines concerned with the human mind and human conduct, which we would call psychology and ethics or moral philosophy.

In treating the part concerned with human beings in association or in society, Bacon used terms for disciplines that we would understand as sociology, economics, and politics (or perhaps as political philosophy) on the one hand, and as the social and behavioral sciences on the other hand. This area he regarded as highly deficient in his own day.

It must be noted that Bacon named metaphysics and mathematics along with physics as the three main branches of natural philosophy. But, as we have already observed, metaphysics as understood by the ancients included what Bacon called *philosophia prima* and also what he called natural or philosophical theology.

An even more questionable point is Bacon's inclusion of mathematics as a subdivision of natural philosophy. Mathematics as understood by the ancients stood apart from physics, as did metaphysics. Neither provided knowledge of natural phenomena. Only physics deals with the realm of becoming—matter in motion and all the phenomena of change. While we today recognize the manifold applications of mathematics in physics and in other natural sciences, we also regard it as a discipline quite distinct from those investigative—empirical or experimental—sciences. Mathematics is neither empirical nor experimental.

Under human philosophy Bacon included what he called the intellectual arts—arts that use the intellect for one purpose or another. In place of what the ancients referred to as the liberal arts and the Middle Ages categorized as the linguistic arts (grammar, rhetoric, and logic) and the mathematical arts (arithmetic, geometry, music, and astronomy), Bacon treated all the intellectual arts as if they were branches of rhetoric and subsumed thereunder both logic and grammar. He entirely omitted the mathematical arts.

Bacon's concern with logic concentrated mainly on the art of discovery, or what we might call the methodology of the empirical or experimental sciences. In this respect he parted company with the traditional conception of the sphere of logic, which is based on Aristotle's *Organon*—his treatise on the subject. That is why Bacon called his treatment of the same subject a *Novum Organum*—a new logic or methodology.

Thomas Hobbes (1588–1679)

The book by Thomas Hobbes in which we find his scheme for the organization of knowledge and his map of human learning is the *Leviathan*, published in 1651. That treatise was primarily a work in political philosophy dealing with the state and man in relation to the state. But in the opening section of the work (which concentrates on the nature of man), Chapter 9, following chapters that deal with the operations of the human mind, is entitled "Of the Several Subjects of Knowledge." Quoting it in its entirety may be the most useful way of introducing the reader to the map or chart of learning that Hobbes presented.

There are of knowledge two kinds, whereof one is knowledge of fact; the other, knowledge of the consequence of one affirmation to another. The former is nothing else but sense and memory, and is *absolute knowledge;* as when we see a fact doing, or remember it done; and this is the knowledge required in a witness. The latter is called *science,* and is conditional; as when we know that: *if the figure shown be a circle, then any straight line through the center shall divide it into two equal parts.* And this is the knowledge required in a philosopher; that is to say, of him that pretends to reasoning.

The register of knowledge of fact is called *history,* whereof there be two sorts: one called *natural history,* which is the history of such facts, or effects of Nature, as have no dependence on man's will; such as are the histories of metals, plants, animals, regions, and the like. The other is *civil history,* which is the history of the voluntary actions of men in Commonwealths.

The registers of science are such books as contain the demonstrations of consequences of one affirmation to another; and are commonly called *books of philosophy;* whereof the sorts are many, according to the diversity of the matter; and may be divided in such manner as I have divided them in the following table. . . .

The table referred to presents a schematic diagram, the overall heading of which is "SCIENCE . . . which is called also PHILOSOPHY." Under this heading, the major division is that between natural philosophy and civil philosophy, or politics.

Natural philosophy includes, first of all, a group of disciplines, the topmost of which is the most general in its consideration of the principles underlying all other disciplines. This, Hobbes, like Bacon, called *philosophia prima*. The other disciplines in this group, less general, include mathematics, cosmography, and mechanics. Mathematics is then subdivided into arithmetic and geometry; cosmography into astronomy and geography; and mechanics into engineering, architecture, and navigation.

What is surprising about this is not that *philosophia prima* and mathematics are here sharply separated from the second main group of disciplines under natural philosophy, but rather that astronomy and engineering are separated from physics, which is the name that Hobbes used to designate the second main group.

In that second group we find not only such special disciplines as meteorology, astrology, and optics, but also music. In addition, and even more surprising, we find ethics, poetry, rhetoric, logic, and jurisprudence.

In all the respects that I have called surprising, Hobbes departs not only from Bacon's more traditional scheme, but also even more so from the maps of knowledge and learning that were dominant in antiquity and the Middle Ages. Hobbes entirely omits theology from his scheme of things, not only excluding divine philosophy, or sacred theology, but also philosophical or natural theology. His subsuming of ethics or moral philosophy under the branch of natural philosophy he calls physics is as unintelligible as his inclusion under the same heading of poetry and of logic and rhetoric. History is nowhere to be found in this map of learning.

The second main subdivision of science or philosophy, which Hobbes called politics, or civil philosophy as distinguished from natural philosophy, deals, of course, with the institutions of the state, with the rights and du-

ties of the sovereign and the rights and duties of subjects. But here we are impelled to ask why ethics (which
certainly treats of rights and duties) and jurisprudence
(which Hobbes called the science of the just and unjust)
should be so sharply separated from politics, appearing
to have no relation to its concern with rights and duties.

Even though Book I of the *Leviathan*, in its treatment
of human nature and the operations of the mind, deals
with matters that we would consider to be psychologi-
cal, psychology is omitted from Hobbes's scheme; and so,
too, is economics, even though wealth and property have
obvious relevance to the subjects treated under the head
of politics or civil philosophy.

John Locke (1632–1704)

Book IV of Locke's great *Essay Concerning Human
Understanding*, published in 1689, contains a chapter
(numbered XXI) entitled "Of the Division of the Sciences."

Its opening paragraph sets forth a threefold division:
the first is concerned with the nature of things and is
called physics or natural philosophy; the second is concerned with human conduct and is called ethics; and the
third is concerned with the use of language and is called
either the doctrine of signs or logic.

As compared with the organization of knowledge and
the mapping of the sphere of learning advanced by Bacon
and Hobbes, Locke's tripartite scheme is both simplistic
and inadequate. That the three disciplines constituting his
scheme represent important and distinct disciplines cannot be questioned. But what about poetry, history, politics, mathematics, metaphysics, and theology? They
cannot be fitted into his scheme.

It is also important to note that Locke adds nothing to

the tripartite scheme that the Roman Stoics thought sufficient when they divided all of human learning into logic, physics, and ethics.

The picture changes remarkably as we turn now from the seventeenth to the eighteenth and nineteenth centuries.

CHAPTER 8

Modern Times: Eighteenth Century

Denis Diderot (1713–1784) and Jean d'Alembert (1717–1783)

PUBLISHED in the years 1751 to 1780, the French *Encyclopédie*, comprising thirty-five volumes, not only undertook to report the state of knowledge in the various arts and sciences, but also to put some order and system into the organization of knowledge. Its editors, Diderot and d'Alembert, were greatly influenced by Francis Bacon, departing from his scheme only in one major respect: They ignored his distinction between human and divine knowledge, including sacred theology under philosophy.

In his own article on encyclopedias, Diderot explained that the word *"encyclopédie"* signified the coverage of all parts of knowledge, encircled systematically and comprehensively. He used Bacon's tripartite division of all the parts of knowledge according to their dependence, respectively, on memory, imagination, and reason. Consequently, history, poetry, and philosophy constitute the three main categories under which knowledge or learning is to be organized. Diderot presented this

[62]

scheme in his Prospectus for the *Encyclopédie*. D'Alembert adopted it with slight changes in the Preliminary Discourse that he wrote for the first volume.

History they subdivided into sacred, civil, and natural. Poetry comprised three kinds: narrative, dramatic, and parabolic—the first concerned with an imaginary past, the second with an imaginary present, and the third with matters abstract or theoretical. But they also extended the word "poetry" to include all the fine arts—music, painting, engraving, and sculpture.

When they came to philosophy, they departed slightly from Bacon's order of the sciences. Bacon had proceeded from God to nature to man. The French encyclopedists reversed the position of nature and man, putting man first and nature second, but like Bacon they gave first place to ontology or metaphysics, or what Bacon had called *philosophia prima*—first philosophy.

For the French encyclopedists, the sciences of man included what we would call psychology, the sciences of communication (the liberal arts of grammar, rhetoric, and logic), and morals or ethics, including here politics, economics, and jurisprudence. They placed mathematics side by side with physics among the sciences of nature. Under the head of physics, they placed astronomy, meteorology, cosmology, botany, mineralogy, and zoology; and under the head of chemistry, chemistry proper, metallurgy, alchemy, and natural magic. They divided mathematics into pure and applied, including under the latter optics, acoustics, and the theory of probability.

Antoine-Augustin Cournot, a French philosopher of their time, criticized the encyclopedists for adopting Bacon's ordering of the parts of knowledge, which did not take into account the advances in scientific research that had been made in the 145 years since Bacon's *Advancement of Learning* was published. Natural history should no longer be separated from the natural sciences in Cournot's view. Botany should be more closely associated with zoology. The theory of probability should belong in the sphere of pure mathematics, rather than along with optics and acoustics in the sphere of applied mathematics.

Immanuel Kant (1724–1804)

Among Kant's predecessors, the philosophers Gottfried Wilhelm Leibniz and Christian Wolff exercised the greatest influence upon him. In the year 1700 Leibniz produced a scheme that was based on the organization of the curriculum in the German universities of his day: theology, jurisprudence, medicine, intellectual philosophy, mathematics, physics, civil or political history, and literary history, or the history of the arts.

Wolff made a threefold division of knowledge into empirical sciences, mathematics, and philosophy or the rational sciences. He divided the empirical sciences into cosmology and psychology; mathematics, into pure and applied; and philosophy, or the rational sciences, into the speculative and the practical. Under the speculative sciences he placed ontology, or *philosophia prima*, cosmology, and psychology; under the practical, logic, ethics, politics, and technology.

We find in Kant's works two somewhat different explicit schemes for the organization of knowledge. One occurs in the Preface to the second edition of his *Critique of Pure Reason*, published in 1787. There Kant separates logic or methodology from all other branches of knowledge, and the latter he divides into the theoretical and the practical. In so doing, he appears to be following Aristotle, as he does also in his threefold division of the theoretical sciences into physics, mathematics, and metaphysics.

In his Preface to a later work, the *Fundamental Principles of the Metaphysics of Ethics,* Kant concerns himself only with philosophy or what he calls "rational knowledge." This he divides into one formal branch, which consists of logic, and two material branches, which consist of physics, or natural philosophy, and ethics, or moral philosophy.

Neither of the Kantian schemes so far presented represent what lies at the heart of his philosophical approach to the whole realm of human knowledge or learning. The most fundamental point for Kant was the differentiation, following Wolff, of the empirical from the rational disciplines. These can be identified with the natural sciences on the one hand, and with mathematics and the branches of philosophy on the other.

However, in one chapter of his *Critique of Pure Reason,* entitled "The Architectonic of Pure Reason," Kant explains that the differentiation of the natural sciences from mathematics turns on the distinction between concepts that have some derivation from experience and concepts that are purely constructions of the intellect.

In the sphere of knowledge that employs concepts derived from experience, Kant's most fundamental distinction is between those that are employed in synthetic judgments *a posteriori* and those that are employed in synthetic judgments *a priori.*

For Kant, the judgment that $7 + 5 = 12$ is synthetic, not analytic: It is not, as others think it to be, a direct consequence of the definition of the terms employed. It is also *a priori,* not *a posteriori*—not based on any process of empirical investigation or research.

What we would call the empirical sciences, natural or

social, would consist for Kant of all the disciplines in which the judgments made are not only synthetic but also *a posteriori*—the results of empirical investigation or research. Contrasted with these are what Kant called the disciplines of rational science, or the branches of philosophy, all of which are constituted by judgments both synthetic and *a priori*, in no way dependent on empirical investigation or research.

Accordingly, such terms as physics or psychology have for Kant a double use. On the one hand, there are empirical physics and empirical psychology, branches of natural science. On the other hand, there are rational physics and rational psychology, branches of what Kant called transcendental philosophy. Kant at first appears to be following Aristotle in making physics, mathematics, and metaphysics the three main branches of speculative knowledge, but his critical philosophy rejects metaphysics as having any claim to validity among the branches of speculative thought. This rejection arose from his insistence that no synthetic *a priori* judgments are possible for the existence of God, the freedom of the will, and the immortality of the soul. How to affirm the existence of God, the freedom of the will, the immortality of the soul, Kant thought are the three main problems of metaphysics.

We are thus left with mathematics, rational physics (or a philosophy of nature), rational psychology (or a philosophy of mind), and rational anthropology (or a philosophy of man), in addition to all the empirical sciences (which also include physics, psychology, and anthropology). But that is not all; for in the sphere of practical as contrasted with speculative knowledge, Kant stoutly defends the validity of ethics, or moral philosophy, as a rational discipline, as well as the validity of politics, or the science of right—rational jurisprudence.

Finally, with Kant there comes into a special prominence a new discipline, which has come to be called epistemology: the theory of knowledge itself. This is the heart of Kant's own critical philosophy, his critique of pure reason. Though two English philosophers, John Locke and David Hume, preceded Kant in an examination of the grounds for certifying or validating what is genuine knowledge as distinct from mere opinion, the prominence of epistemology in modern philosophical thought stems from him.

It might be more to the point to say the *predominance* of epistemology rather than its prominence, since, in the centuries following Kant, modern epistemology has not only tended to reject metaphysics as a valid branch of knowledge, but has also replaced metaphysics as the reigning regulative discipline.

CHAPTER 9

Modern Times:
Nineteenth Century

Samuel Taylor Coleridge (1772–1834)

LIKE the French encyclopedists of the century before, Coleridge was deeply impressed by the Baconian scheme for the organization of knowledge. He did not follow it, however, as closely as the encyclopedists did. The table of arrangement he drew up in 1817 for his projected *Encyclopedia Metropolitana* was presented in his "Treatise on Method," which was published in the first volume of that encyclopedia in the following year. Coleridge's classification and ordering of the branches of knowledge was somewhat altered later by the publishers of his encyclopedia.

His table of arrangement was comprised of four divisions. Of these the first consisted of the pure sciences, subdivided into the formal and the real. The formal sciences consisted of universal grammar or philology, logic, and mathematics. The real sciences, or the sciences of reality, consisted of metaphysics, morals, and theology.

Coleridge subdivided the second main division into the mixed and applied sciences. The mixed sciences consisted of mechanics, hydraulics, pneumatics, optics, and astronomy. The applied sciences were broken down into five subdivisions: 1) the branches of experimental philosophy—magnetism, electricity, chemistry, light, heat, color, and meteorology; 2) the fine arts—poetry, painting, sculpture, and architecture; 3) the useful arts—agriculture, commerce, and manufactures; 4) natural history—physiology, crystallography, geology, mineralogy, botany, and zoology; and 5) the applications of natural history—anatomy, surgery, *materia medica*, pharmacy, and medicine.

Articles treating the first two of Coleridge's main divisions of knowledge were to occupy the first eight volumes of the *Encyclopedia Metropolitana*, with articles on subjects in the second division filling six of these eight volumes.

The historical, biographical, and geographical articles that constituted Coleridge's third main division were planned for the next eight volumes. Remaining for the last eight volumes were the kind of articles that we would include in a lexicon or in a gazetteer, the entries in which would be alphabetically arranged, the whole to be followed by an alphabetical index.

The *Encyclopedia Metropolitana* was never completed according to Coleridge's plan, which employed a combination of systematic and alphabetical principles for the organization of an encyclopedia, the first eight volumes being purely topical or systematic in the arrangement of its articles, the last twenty being alphabetical.

The *Encyclopaedia Britannica*, which in its first edition (1769) was purely alphabetical and has remained so in all of its fifteen editions, has survived for more than two hundred years. In contrast, the partly topical *Encyclopedia Metropolitana* was an impressive failure. It did not long remain in print. Probably it failed because the topical arrangement of its articles on the major arts and sciences did not serve the purposes of readers who wanted to use an encyclopedia solely as a reference work and not as a systematic survey of all the major fields of learning. Nevertheless, subsequent editors of alphabetical encyclopedias, including *Britannica,* were influenced by Coleridge's main categories for the branches of knowledge.

In the nineteenth and even the twentieth centuries, encyclopedia editors used such categories to classify the articles they sought from their contributors, even though, when the articles came in, they placed them in a purely alphabetical order.

An example of this is to be found in the Classified Table of Contents of the eleventh edition of *Encyclopaedia Britannica* (a copy of which can be found in Chapter 2). Unlike Coleridge's chart of categories, which was not alphabetically arranged, *Britannica's* Classified Table of Contents was purely alphabetical.

André Marie Ampère (1775–1836)

Toward the close of his life, the French scientist-philosopher Ampère published a treatise, the title of which translated into English runs as follows: *An essay on the philosophy of the sciences; or an analytical exposition of a natural classification of the whole of human knowledge.*

Therein the branches of knowledge were ordered in a manner that has a typically modern ring: mathematics, physics and other natural sciences, medicine, the branches of philosophy, literature and pedagogy, ethnology, and the political sciences.

Expanded somewhat, mathematics for Ampère consisted of arithmetic and geometry; under or associated with physics were mechanics, kinematics, dynamics, astronomy, geology, botany, zoology, and agriculture; medicine carried with it pharmacy and hygenics.

Auguste Comte (1798–1857)

According to Auguste Comte, progress in human learning proceeds through three stages. The first stage is that of theology, or what for Comte amounts to mythology or superstition. The second stage is that of metaphysics, or speculative philosophy. This for Comte consists of abstract speculation and unfounded theory. Finally, in the modern era, we reach at last the stage of empirically certified valid knowledge, represented by the positive sciences.

It was this picture of the history of human thought that branded Comte as the founder of positivism, which has taken many forms in the nineteenth and twentieth centuries and is especially prevalent in our own day.

The word "positive" characterizes all genuine knowledge as distinct from mere opinion. It is knowledge based on fact. It is not speculation or theorizing, up in the air with no feet on the ground. It is empirical or experimental in method, starting from observed facts and returning to observed facts for verification. It deals only with observable phenomena.

These strictures make it difficult to understand how Comte justified including mathematics along with the empirical or experimental sciences. Pure mathematics is neither an empirical nor an experimental science. Comte's only ground for doing so was his recognition of the role that mathematics played in the development of the natural sciences, especially celestial and terrestrial mechanics, the first branches of mathematical physics to emerge in modern times. Comte was obviously unaware that the Alexandrian scientists of antiquity, in both astronomy and mechanics, were also mathematical physicists.

Comte's sixfold division of the positive sciences is ordered according to the degree of simplicity and complexity of the phenomena being investigated, and also the relative abstractness and concreteness of the objects being studied. This gives us the following arrangement of all the disciplines that exhaustively constitute the domain of genuine learning: mathematics, astronomy, physics, chemistry, biology and physiology, and sociology, or what Comte also called social philosophy.

Comte's further subdivision of these six main departments of scientific knowledge need not be considered here, in view of the tremendous advances in science since his day, and the vast proliferation of specialized disciplines under each of his main headings. Of much greater significance are the omissions or eliminations from the field of learning that characterize Comte's positivist approach to the organization of knowledge.

First of all is the elimination on principle not only of theoretical or speculative philosophy (metaphysics, the philosophy of nature, and the philosophy of mind), but also of practical philosophy (ethics and politics). Then there is the omission, with no reasons given, of history, both political and cultural. Finally, there is no mention of poetry and of other fine arts, nor is there any consideration of the traditional liberal arts of grammar, rhetoric, and logic.

Under sociology or social philosophy, Comte included such disciplines as political science, political economy, and social but not physical anthropology; and he would appear to have no place for empirical psychology, both human and animal, as a behavioral science.

Wilhelm Dilthey (1833–1911)

Significantly different from the other modern schemes for the organization of knowledge we have so far examined is Dilthey's division of learning into two major fields: 1) the natural sciences, both those concerned with non-human phenomena and those concerned with man's mental processes and behavior; and 2) the humanities, which, for Dilthey, included history and biography, economics, politics, and law, moral philosophy or ethics, religion, poetry, architecture, and music.

This basic twofold division is probably more accurately expressed by the German words *"Naturwissenschaften"* and *"Geisteswissenschaften."* The second of Dilthey's main divisions—poorly designated by the English word "humanities"—is further subdivided according to the method or manner in which the objects considered are studied. On the one hand, there is the historical approach to the study of economics and politics, or of man's moral and social life. On the other hand, there is the systematic approach to the same subjects, in such disciplines as economics, sociology, and psychology, or in moral and political philosophy. So, too, poetry can be studied historically, or it can be approached systematically in literary criticism.

Herbert Spencer (1820–1903)

Spencer, like Comte, proposed a systematic ordering of what he regarded in his day as acknowledged sciences or disciplines. Unlike Comte, he was not a positivist. He did not exclude from the field of learning the whole of philosophy, for he himself attempted to make contributions to moral philosophy or ethics. Nor did he exclude disciplines that were partly scientific and partly philosophical. However, like Comte, he gave little or no consideration to history or poetry and other arts.

His principle for ordering the sciences was in terms of their relative abstractness or concreteness. Thus he placed logic and mathematics first as purely abstract disciplines. Next came mechanics, physics, and chemistry as sciences both abstract and concrete. These were followed by the purely concrete sciences of astronomy, geology, biology, psychology, and sociology.

Both Comte's and Spencer's schemes for the organization of knowledge have the aspect of museum pieces. They have more interest as matters of historical record than as significant for us today. Unlike the map or chart of all human learning laid down by Francis Bacon, and adopted with modifications by the French encyclopedists and others, the schemes of Comte and Spencer are not sufficiently comprehensive. The principles they employ in drawing up these schemes are much more challengeable than those employed by Bacon.

PART THREE
CONTEMPORARY EFFORTS TO ORGANIZE KNOWLEDGE

CHAPTER 10

A Twentieth-Century Proposal

A SURVEY of attempts to map or chart the realm of learning would be incomplete if some characteristically twentieth-century efforts were not included. In this and the next two chapters I will give a brief account of them and explain why they do not deliver the guidance that is needed.

At the beginning of this century, a number of books appeared that addressed themselves to the problem of classifying library books in terms of the organization of knowledge. Three were written by Americans: *Classification, Theoretical and Practical*, by E. C. Richardson in 1930; *The Organization of Knowledge and the System of the Sciences*, by H. E. Bliss in 1929; and *The Organization of Knowledge in Libraries*, also by Bliss, 1933. It must be added that these American efforts were influenced by an earlier British book on library arrangement—*Manual of Classification and Shelf Arrangement*, by J. D. Brown, published in 1898.

Richardson's scheme was governed by his explicitly stated principle that "the order of the sciences is the order of things" and by his declaration that "the order of things is lifeless, living, human, and superhuman," thus going from the sciences of the inanimate to the sciences

THE ORDER OF NATURE	THE PEDAGOGIC ORDER	THE LOGICAL ORDER
Substance, Matter, Reality	Science and Philosophy	Science and Philosophy
Media (aetherial, electronic, and other)	Natural Science	Natural Science
	Applied Mechanics,	Physics
Energy, Relations	Engineering	Chemistry
Physical Actions and States	Chemical Science	Special Natural Sciences
	Astronomy	
Chemical Elements and Actions	Geology	Astronomy
		Geology
Bodies, Structures (inorganic)	Biology, Botany, Zoology	Biology
Organisms	Anthropology	Anthropology
Mind	Psychology	Psychology
Societies, Communities, Ethnic Groups, Social Groups	Social Sciences, Sociology	Education
		Sociology
	Aesthetics, Technologies	Arts (fine, useful, recreative)
	Philology	
		Philology

dealing with living organisms, and then to the sciences or disciplines dealing with human life and society, leaving religion or theology to the last.

While the system of the positive sciences proposed by Bliss closely resembles that proposed by Auguste Comte (mathematics, physics, chemistry, biology, anthropology, and sociology), his overall view of the field of learning included much more than that list of the positive sciences. It included philosophy, history, geography, religion, politics, and the fine arts.

For Bliss, the four basic areas of human knowledge consist of philosophy, science, history, technology, and the arts. His book on the organization of knowledge contains a number of synoptic tables, constructed differently on the basis of different principles. One is constructed in accordance with the order of nature; another sets forth the pedagogical order in which things should be studied; and still another, the logical order of the subject matters to be studied.

In my judgment, these three synoptic tables are of sufficient interest to be reproduced in part. Readers need only glance at these to perceive quickly their general tenor.

In 1970, Bliss revised the system of bibliographic classification that he first presented in 1933. Here is a synopsis of its main headings:

Philosophy (its branches and its history, both Eastern and Western)	History
	Religion
Logic	Social Welfare
Mathematics	Political Science

Statistics and Probability	Public Administration
Physical Science and Technology	Law
Biological Sciences	Economics
Anthropology	Finance, Banking, and Insurance
Medicine	
	Technology and Useful Arts
Psychology	
Education	Fine Arts
Social Sciences	Philology

The foregoing system of bibliographic classification (here presented with some abbreviation) must be considered in its own terms and in the light of its own purposes. It is a scheme for putting books on the shelves of libraries in an orderly fashion, better in some respects than either the Dewey Decimal System or that of the Library of Congress. It is certainly more instructive than the purely alphabetical ordering of departments in a college or university catalogue, or of the articles in an alphabetically organized encyclopedia. However, it falls far short of the enlightenment or understanding that should result from a map or chart of learning based on explicitly declared philosophical principles.

Such maps or charts existed in antiquity and in the Middle Ages (see chapters 5 and 6), and also in modern times, especially in the works of Bacon, Kant, and Coleridge (see chapters 7, 8, and 9). However, none of these are wholly acceptable to us or appropriate for us in the twentieth century.

They contain some insights and some distinctions that still have relevance for us and provide us with some guidance. But the task of mapping or charting the whole sphere of knowledge and the realm of human learning remains to be done in a manner that is acceptable and appropriate today.

Two steps in that direction, in both of which I have been involved, deserve to be considered before I undertake to tackle the task that remains. One is the construction of the Propaedia, or Outline of Knowledge, published along with the fifteenth edition of the *Encyclopaedia Britannica* in 1974, and improved in the 1985 edition. The other is the Syntopicon, which was an index of the great ideas, published along with *Great Books of the Western World* in 1952. These two steps will be reported in chapters 11 and 12 to follow.

CHAPTER 11

The Propaedia

DURING the twenty-five years between 1949 and 1974, when Robert M. Hutchins was chairman of the Board of Editors of the *Encyclopaedia Britannica*, the most insistent and vexatious problem discussed at board meetings was the choice between an alphabetical and a topical organization for the next edition.

In its first fourteen editions the *Britannica* had been alphabetically organized in a single series of article titles from A to Z. The first edition in 1768 did, however, make a clear typographical distinction between the short entries in that one alphabetical series, entries having purely informational content, and the long articles or essays that provided expositions of the major fields of knowledge or learning.

Throughout the 1950s and in the early 1960s, the Board of Editors was charged with planning a new *Britannica*—a fifteenth edition. Faced with that task, its members, in session after session, debated the merits of a topical as opposed to an alphabetical arrangement of articles.

At that time, the only topically organized encyclopedia we could consult in order to weigh the pros and cons of the issue was the *Encyclopédie française*. Its table of

contents is worth examining here as background for what
is to follow.

As originally projected, its twenty-one volumes were
to bear the following titles.

I.	Thought, Language, Mathematics
II.	Problems of Physics
III.	The Universe and the Planet Earth
IV.	Life
V.	Living Beings
VI.	The Human Being
VII.	The Human Species
VIII.	The Stages of Humanity
IX.	The Legacy of the Past to the Present
X.	The Modern State
XI.	The States of the World
XII.	Economic Organization (1)
XIII.	Economic Organization (2)
XIV.	Well-being and Culture
XV.	Intellectual Life and Education
XVI.	Art and Literature (1)
XVII.	Art and Literature (2)
XVIII.	Religion and Philosophies
XIX.	Man, Earth, Machine
XX.	Bibliography and List of Proper Names
XXI.	Alphabetical List of Subjects

It will be noted at once that, although history is treated
at considerable length, neither biography nor geography
receive explicit treatment. Volume I, after a general introduction, is divided into three parts: 1) the evolution
of thought, primitive and logical; 2) language, dealing with
the structure of linguistic data, the types of languages, and

alphabets and writing systems; and 3) the various branches of mathematics.

Volume II has three parts, the first dealing with mechanics, electromagnetics, and thermodynamics; the second, with the atomic sciences; the third with relativity, wave mechanics, radiation, and nuclear physics.

Volume III, dealing with the heavens and the Earth, devotes the section on the heavens to the Solar System, the sun and other stars, the galaxies, and the problems of cosmic evolution. The section on the Earth treats the terrestrial globe, the crust of the Earth and its topography.

Volume IV is divided into five parts: 1) the origins of life; 2) the physical structure and chemical composition of living matter; 3) the organization of living beings; 4) cellular activities; and 5) the sustenance and survival of animals.

Volume V deals first with flora and fauna, plants and animals; and then in a second part treats the distribution of living beings.

Volume VI considers first the physical life of man in normal health; and then, in the second part, treats human illness—diseases, the present state of the higher medical disciplines, and the practice of medicine.

Volume VII, concerned with the human species, has three divisions: anthropology, ethnography, and ethnology—the first considering the diversity of human groups; the second, peoples and races; and the third, population and sexuality.

Volume VIII, concerned with the stages of humanity, covers the study of human character and psychoanalysis.

Volume IX deals with the social and economic world, covering statistical data, the dynamics of social development, the operations of economics, the distribution of wealth, the satisfaction of human needs and the costs thereof, economic problems and issues, and the emergence of a new economy.

Volume X, on the state, has five sections: 1) the history of the state; 2) political data; 3) political institutions; 4) political activities; and 5) international relations.

Volume XI, on international affairs, considers the sources of international conflict, lines that cross international borders, the blocs of nations, and the world scene.

Volume XII treats chemistry, first considering chemistry as a science, then the human significance of chemistry, and finally the chemistry of human beings.

Volume XIII deals with industry and agriculture, treating the technology of each and the human uses of each.

Volume XIV is concerned with everyday life. It considers man's daily life, the organization of human space, living quarters, nutrition, clothing, and entertainment.

Volume XV, which covers education and instruction, first considers the types of teaching in countries having liberal traditions and institutions, then teaching in three European dictatorships and also in countries outside of Europe. It goes on to report pedagogical methods and cultural objectives, and finally it takes up a number of political and social problems affecting education.

Volumes XVI and XVII are entitled art and literature, respectively. Despite that general heading for the two volumes, the first of these deals with the worker and the consumer; the second, with the interaction of the worker and the consumer.

Volume XVIII, concerned with the role of writing in civilized nations, treats first the graphic arts, then the importance of books, their publication and distribution, then magazines and newspapers, and finally libraries.

Volume XIX is on philosophies and religions. The part dealing with philosophies treats the principal trends of contemporary philosophy, including the state of current philosophical problems and the means of their solution; it concludes with an exposition of philosophical doctrines. The part dealing with religions has three sections: the phenomonology of religions; the history and sociology of religion; and the spirit of contemporary religions.

Finally, Volume XX undertakes to consider the emerging world—its history, its evolution, and its future.

This description of the contents of the twenty volumes departs in many instances from the table of contents laid down when the encyclopedia was first projected. For one reason or another, the editors found themselves obliged to change course as the work proceeded volume by volume.

This indicates one embarrassment that seems inescapable in the progressive construction of a topical encyclopedia. Another arises from the conflict between the pedagogical ordering of the subjects to be considered and the logical arrangement of subject matters or of the various departments of knowledge. It is apparent that the editors of the *Encyclopédie française* shifted from one focus to the other, not only in the succession of volumes, but also in the structuring of each volume. In addition, questions arise concerning matters omitted, overlooked, or given only passing or subordinate treatment in contrast to subjects that occupy the center of the stage.*

---

* The Chinese are currently engaged in producing a great encyclopedia, the first (in a strict use of the word "encyclopedia") in the Chinese language. One part of it is alphabetical, consisting in a translation, with minor modifications, of *Britannica*'s Micropaedia (volumes of short informational entries). The other part will consist of some seventy volumes, topically arranged, each treating a whole department or province of knowledge or learning. This work has only just begun and therefore it is impossible to report the subject matters to be successively covered in these seventy or more volumes. But there can be little

All of these embarrassments and questions connected with the planning and execution of a topically organized encyclopedia came to the attention of the *Britannica's* Board of Editors as they weighed the pros and cons of topical versus alphabetical organization. How long the debate would have gone on and how it would have been decided remains in doubt, for the issue was decided for the Board of Editors by Senator William Benton, the publisher of the encyclopedia and chairman of the Board of Directors of Encyclopaedia Britannica, Inc.

Benton attended the editorial meetings. He declined to take the risk of a commercial failure that might result from publishing a topical encyclopedia. Coleridge's *Encyclopedia Metropolitana* had experienced such a failure in the nineteenth century, and the history of the *Encyclopédie française* gave no assurance that matters stood otherwise in the twentieth century. There appeared to be no sizeable market for an encyclopedia that did not easily serve the wishes of those who purchased encyclopedias as reference works for the purpose of looking things up, a purpose much more readily served by an alphabetical than by a topical arrangement of articles, even if the latter is accompanied by an alphabetically organized index of subjects.

At one point in the ongoing discussion, the chairman of the Board of Editors, Mr. Hutchins, proposed a compromise. He suggested dividing the whole encyclopedia into two subsets of volumes. One subset would provide information about the particulars of persons, places, and things—the biographical and geographical articles, and an account of particular institutions, events, and objects.

---

doubt that, when completed, the same embarrassments and difficult questions will have emerged.

The other subset would provide the coverage of the major subjects in all departments of knowledge and in all fields of art, science, and scholarship. The first subset would be alphabetically arranged for the look-it-up purpose; the second would be topically arranged for those who wished to study a whole area of subject matter.

This suggestion was also rejected. It emerged once again after the fifteenth edition had been completed and published in 1974, at a time when I, having succeeded Robert Hutchins as chairman of the Board of Editors, proposed this plan for another new edition of the encyclopedia. It was once again rejected by the Board and by the management of the company.

I had been a member of the Board of Editors since its inception in 1949, and I became director of editorial planning for the fifteenth edition of *Britannica* in 1965. One innovative change in the plan that was finally adopted derived from those earlier editorial deliberations. This was the proposed division of the volumes of the encyclopedia into two subsets: one containing a large number of relatively short entries having mainly informational content, the other containing a very small number of relatively long articles, essays on the major subjects in all fields of knowledge. Both series of articles—the short ones comprising the "Micropaedia" and the long ones in "Macropaedia"—were to be alphabetically arranged.

That change in the fifteenth edition, though a radical departure, did in fact reflect the typographical distinction in *Britannica's* first edition between the short informational entries and the long scholarly essays expounding the state of organized knowledge. The execution of this part of the plan has been completed in the 1985 revision of the fifteenth edition.

The other radical innovation that emerged in the planning for the fifteenth edition attempted to resolve the issue of topical versus alphabetical arrangement. Given the unalterable decision that articles had to be alphabetically arranged and their subject matter alphabetically indexed, we invented a device whereby the reader would be given a topical as well as an alphabetical mode of access to the contents of the encyclopedia.

That device took the form of an outline of knowledge that would be both a scheme for editing the fifteenth edition in a more intelligible and systematic fashion than any alphabetical encyclopedia had been previously edited, and also an analytical Table of Contents for the use of those readers who wished to study in a protracted manner some whole field of subject matter or some department of learning. Because we thought this proposed outline of knowledge would serve as a readable introduction to the encyclopedia as a whole, we called the volume that contained it the "Propaedia."

Planning it as a Table of Contents for the long articles in the Macropaedia, we affixed page references to the thousands of topics enumerated in the Outline of Knowledge. We subsequently improved the Propaedia by removing these page references and turning the Propaedia into an elaborate study guide, or set of study guides. In each of the 186 sections of the Outline of Knowledge we eliminated all page references and replaced them with the titles of articles in both the Macropaedia and the Micropaedia recommended as relevant to the topics covered in each section of the Outline. This improvement of the Propaedia first appeared in 1985.

The initial construction of the Outline of Knowledge took eight years of work, involving the senior members of the *Britannica*'s editorial staff under the supervision of Philip Goetz, then *Britannica*'s executive editor, now its editor-in-chief. It also involved consultation with academic specialists in all the fields of knowledge and learning covered in the outline.

It is important to stress the fact that the production of the Propaedia was a vast collaborative effort. In that respect, the Propaedia's map or chart of the whole realm of human learning differs from all the maps or charts presented in the preceding chapters, especially those produced from the seventeenth century on, all of which were the work of individuals.

Before I set forth a synopsis of the Outline of Knowledge as it appeared in the 1985 version of the Propaedia, I must call attention to one fact about the order of its ten parts. Here are the ten parts as entitled:

Part One.	Matter and Energy
Part Two.	The Earth
Part Three.	Life on Earth
Part Four.	Human Life
Part Five.	Human Society
Part Six.	Art
Part Seven.	Technology
Part Eight.	Religion
Part Nine.	The History of Mankind
Part Ten.	The Branches of Knowledge

My preface to the Propaedia, entitled "The Circle of Learning," pointed out that these ten parts were not to be thought of as arranged in an ascending or descending linear order, nor arranged in a hierarchical fashion, going from what is more fundamental to what is less fundamental, or from what is simple to what is more complex; and certainly not in an order that was either primarily logical or primarily pedagogical.

I explained the reason for this. We live in an age and in a society that is dominated by cultural pluralism and intellectual heterodoxy. Unacceptable, therefore, would

be any ordering of the departments of knowledge or the
fields of learning that is hierarchical or that is ascending
or descending in a scale of values involving judgments
about what is more or less fundamental, important, or
significant, or about what should be studied from first to
last for logical or pedagogical reasons. Such an ordering
would be regarded as culturally monolithic instead of
pluralistic, or as the expression of an orthodoxy that was
purely subjective instead of accommodating the prevalent intellectual heterodoxy. It would be challenged at
every point as being opinionated in a privately tenden- *biased*
tious manner instead of representing, as it should, a public consensus. A "ladder" of learning is therefore ruled
out. All parts of learning must be treated coordinately as
if they were all placed in relation to one another like
points on a circle.

The same embarrassments and difficulties that were
unavoidable in the construction of a purely topical encyclopedia, such as the *Encyclopédie française,* would
plague the construction of a topical outline of knowledge that involved the kind of value judgments entering
into any hierarchical ordering of departments of knowledge or fields of learning.

For all these reasons, I declared that the ten parts of
the outline of knowledge formed a circle, in which no
part came first and none came last. Each of the ten parts
could be a starting point from which one might move in
any direction to other parts of the circle. Each part might
be placed at the center of the circle, as a focus from which
one could move out along one radius after another to the
remaining nine parts on the periphery of the circle.

The whole of the Propaedia's synoptic outline of
knowledge deserves to be read carefully. It represents a
twentieth-century scheme for the organization of knowledge that is more comprehensive than any other and that

also accommodates the intellectual heterodoxy of our time. I have placed it in Appendix I, to which I hope readers will turn with a special interest after they have read the concluding paragraphs of this book.

Here I wish only to have readers look at Part Ten of this outline, entitled "The Branches of Knowledge." It consists of five divisions, as follows.

```
  I.   Logic
         History and Philosophy of Logic
         Formal Logic, Metalogic, and Applied Logic
 II.   Mathematics
         History and Foundations of Mathematics
         Branches of Mathematics
         Applications of Mathematics
III.   Science
         History and Philosophy of Science
         The Physical Sciences
         The Earth Sciences
         The Biological Sciences
         Medicine and Affiliated Disciplines
         The Social Sciences and Psychology
         The Technological Sciences
 IV.   History and the Humanities
         Historiography and the Study of History
         The Humanities and Humanistic Scholarship
  V.   Philosophy
         History of Philosophy
         The Nature and Divisions of Philosophy
         Philosophical Schools and Doctrines
```

This ordering of the branches of knowledge calls for a number of critical comments.

One lies in the fact that Part Ten differs radically from the other nine parts. The first nine parts cover knowledge about the world of nature and of man. The topics there set forth indicate the learning we can acquire from the scientists and the scholars who, in their respective disciplines, study the phenomena of nature, of human life, and of human society—its institutions, arts, technology, religions, and history. In sharp contrast the tenth part (with three exceptions to be noted presently) deals with the disciplines themselves, the various branches of knowledge—their scope, history, methods, subdivisions, and problems.

The three exceptions are the divisions of Part Ten entitled "Logic," "Mathematics," and "Philosophy." The opening sections of each of these three divisions deal with the nature of these disciplines in themselves: their scope, history, and methods. But the remaining sections in each case set forth the knowledge or learning that can be acquired from studying logic, mathematics, and philosophy. They set forth the doctrines and theories of logic, mathematics, and philosophy, just as the other nine parts set forth the doctrines and theories of physics, astronomy, chemistry, the earth sciences, biology, psychology, the social sciences, and so on.

That being the case, we are faced with the question whether it was proper to place logic, mathematics, and philosophy in Part Ten along with the treatment of the other branches of knowledge, the doctrines and theories of which are covered in the first nine parts.

Logic and mathematics have special objects of study—purely intelligible objects that have no existence in the physical world. In sharp contrast, the empirical sciences, natural and social, explore and study the phenomenal world of real existence. Like logic and mathematics, some branches of philosophy also treat

purely intelligible objects, but other branches of philosophy have objects that are the same as the objects studied in the empirical sciences, although studied there by
methods distinctly different from the methods of philosophy. This makes the placement in Part Ten of philosophy, along with logic and mathematics and other branches
of knowledge, peculiarly troublesome.

There is an additional difficulty about philosophy. At
certain places in the first nine parts, we find such topics
as the philosophy of law, the philosophy of education,
the philosophy of art, and so on. A similar difficulty arises
with respect to history. Part Nine is devoted to the history of mankind, but that is mainly social and political
history. Most of cultural and intellectual history is to be
found in the other parts; e.g., the history of legal systems, the history of education, the history of each of the
fine arts, and so on, in Parts One through Nine of the
outline; and the history of logic, of mathematics, of philosophy, and of the various empirical sciences and other
fields of scholarship, in Part Ten.

These difficulties raise questions about the very special character of philosophy and history in the whole
range of disciplines. I shall return to these questions in
Chapter 14. The discussion of this matter will have great
significance for a final attempt to provide the kind of
guidance that I have promised my readers.

One more serious defect in the Propaedia's Outline of
Knowledge remains to be considered. Being an outline
of the kinds of knowledge or the departments of learning
that can properly be covered in a general encyclopedia,
the encyclopedic treatment of philosophy is necessarily
restricted to the exposition of the doctrines and theories
that are taught to students in the academy by professors
of philosophy. But such academic or professional philosophy (I am tempted to say "professorial philosophy")

is not philosophy for the layman—the kind of philosophy which is, or should be, everybody's business.

Philosophy, so conceived, consists in the understanding of the great ideas that provide the underlying principles and governing insights in every field of subject matter. The generalist's approach to the study of the arts and sciences and the various departments of scholarship must be in terms of the basic principles and governing insights that derive from an understanding of these ideas.

An adequate treatment of the great ideas is not to be found in an encyclopedia. An encyclopedia provides its readers with information and the organized knowledge that results from scientific research and scholarly inquiry. It does not include philosophical understanding or poetic insights, and certainly does not provide speculative or practical wisdom.

We must look elsewhere for a thorough examination and clarification of the great ideas and of the issues and controversies that revolve around them. We must turn from the Propaedia's Outline of Knowledge, knowledge that is properly covered in an encyclopedia, to *Great Books of the Western World* if we are to consider the significance of the great ideas for a guidebook to learning.

As the Propaedia's Outline of Knowledge stands in relation to the *Encyclopaedia Britannica*, so the Syntopicon's enumeration of the great ideas and its essays on each of them stand in relation to *Great Books of the Western World*. What the Syntopicon can do for us in this guide book to learning is the subject of the following chapter.

The Syntopicon

Great Books of the Western World had its inception at the University of Chicago when Robert Hutchins was president of the university and I was a member of the faculty. The instigation of the project came from William Benton in 1943, the same year that he became the publisher of *Encyclopaedia Britannica*.

After eight years of work, involving the collaboration of many scholars, that set of books was published in 1952 with Hutchins as Editor-in-Chief and myself as Associate Editor. I was, in addition, responsible for the production of the Syntopicon that accompanied the *Great Books* and served as an instrument for locating passages in them where their authors discussed the topics that constituted the inner structure of the great ideas. Because it was organized around three thousand topics under 102 great ideas, that instrument, occupying two volumes in the set, came to be called *The Great Ideas, or Syntopicon* (the coined word "syntopicon" meaning a collection of topics).

The selection of the authors and works to comprise *Great Books* was carried out by an editorial committee over a period of three years. The production of the Syntopicon was the work of an editorial staff numbering more than thirty-five persons and involved 400,000 man-hours of reading over the course of six years. This endeavor did not begin until two years had been spent in determining which ideas were "great" in the sense of being major centers of discussion and controversy throughout the twenty-five-century span of Western civilization. Indexing the intellectual content of 443 works by seventy-four authors stretching across twenty-five centuries from Homer to Freud was, to say the least, a challenging task.

Just as the Propaedia functions to give readers topical access to the information and organized knowledge contained in the encyclopedia, so the Syntopicon functions to provide readers with topical access to the ideas discussed in the *Great Books*. The problem confronted in the editing of the Syntopicon was the same as that faced in the editing of the Propaedia.

In the latter case, as we have seen, the question was: How should the ten parts of the Outline of Knowledge be organized—in a linear, ascending, or descending fashion, or in a circle that allowed each of the ten parts to be considered as coordinate with all the others?

In the case of the Syntopicon we faced a similar question: How should the 102 great ideas be set forth—with some given precedence or priority over others in terms of an evaluation of their degree of greatness, or treated as coordinate with one another, none subordinate, none supraordinate?

Our decision was the same in both cases and for the same reason. The pluralistic culture and the intellectual heterodoxy of the twentieth century, we felt, would not tolerate the kind of value judgments involved in a hierarchical ordering of either the great ideas or the parts of knowledge. An individual author, signing his name to a book he has himself written, might be in a position to argue for or defend value judgments of this kind; but a work produced by the collaborative effort of many persons, such as the Propaedia and the Syntopicon, does not have that option. Hence the 102 great ideas were presented in strictly alphabetical order, and the Great Books themselves were presented in a sequence roughly determined by the chronological order of their authors' lives.

Could anything be done to introduce some ordering of both the books and the ideas in a more significant and intelligible fashion than one determined alphabetically or chronologically? That question is relevant to our present concerns, for only when we depart from or transcend such intellectually neutral orderings as those provided by alphabetization and chronology do we begin to see guidelines for the pursuit of learning.

Our solution of this problem with regard to the Great Books was accomplished by dividing the authors into four main groups, and then indicating such grouping by placing swatches of different color on the backbones of the volumes that contained their works.

A yellow swatch indicated works of imaginative literature—epic and dramatic poetry, novels and plays, and, in the case of Shakespeare's and Milton's sonnets, lyric poetry as well. A green swatch indicated works in the fields of mathematics, astronomy, physics, chemistry, biology, psychology, and medicine. A blue swatch indicated histories, biographies, and treatises in the fields of political theory and economics. A red swatch indicated works in philosophy and theology—metaphysics, the philosophy of nature, the philosophy of mind, and both natural and sacred theology.

This classification of the volumes in Great Books of the Western World could not be perfectly precise, because where the volumes contained all the works of certain authors, or even several of them, placing that author in one of these four groups had to ignore the fact that some of his writings may belong in one group and some in another. His being placed in one group rather than another could be defended only in terms of the predominant character of his contribution to the tradition of Western culture.

Before I turn to the way in which we attempted to solve the same problem with regard to the great ideas, in order to offset or overcome the neutrality of their alphabetical enumeration, I think it useful to give the reader that alphabetical listing first. Here it is.

ANGEL	FAMILY	MATHEMATICS
ANIMAL	FATE	MATTER
ARISTOCRACY	FORM	MECHANICS
ART	GOD	MEDICINE
ASTRONOMY	GOOD AND EVIL	MEMORY AND
BEAUTY	GOVERNMENT	IMAGINATION
BEING	HABIT	METAPHYSICS
CAUSE	HAPPINESS	MIND
CHANCE	HISTORY	MONARCHY
CHANGE	HONOR	NATURE
CITIZEN	HYPOTHESIS	NECESSITY AND
CONSTITUTION	IDEA	CONTINGENCY
COURAGE	IMMORTALITY	OLIGARCHY
CUSTOM AND	INDUCTION	ONE AND MANY
CONVENTION	INFINITY	OPINION
DEFINITION	JUDGMENT	OPPOSITION
DEMOCRACY	JUSTICE	PHILOSOPHY
DESIRE	KNOWLEDGE	PHYSICS
DIALECTIC	LABOR	PLEASURE AND PAIN
DUTY	LANGUAGE	POETRY
EDUCATION	LAW	PRINCIPLE
ELEMENT	LIBERTY	PROGRESS
EMOTION	LIFE AND DEATH	PROPHECY
ETERNITY	LOGIC	PRUDENCE
EVOLUTION	LOVE	PUNISHMENT
EXPERIENCE	MAN	QUALITY

QUANTITY	SIN	UNIVERSAL AND
REASONING	SLAVERY	PARTICULAR
RELATION	SOUL	VIRTUE AND VICE
RELIGION	SPACE	WAR AND PEACE
REVOLUTION	STATE	WEALTH
RHETORIC	TEMPERANCE	WILL
SAME AND OTHER	THEOLOGY	WISDOM
SCIENCE	TIME	WORLD
SENSE	TRUTH	
SIGN AND SYMBOL	TYRANNY	

Is that list, as drawn up in the 1940s, satisfactory to-day? Should any ideas be added to it? I have only three nominations now for additions to the 102. I think the omission of Equality should be corrected, and perhaps also the omission of Power and Property. Equality certainly belongs in the list along with Liberty. Property may already be sufficiently covered in connection with Wealth; and the same may be said about Power in connection with State, Government, and Tyranny.

Examination of the 102 great ideas as alphabetically listed will reveal that the list includes twelve ideas that stand out as different from all the rest. In alphabetical order they are: Art, Astronomy, History, Mechanics, Medicine, Metaphysics, Philosophy, Physics, Poetry, Religion, Science, Theology. If readers recall the difference between Part Ten in the Propaedia, concerned with the branches of knowledge, and parts One through Nine, which cover what we know about the world by means of these various branches of knowledge, they will see that the same difference exists between the special set of twelve ideas named above and all the rest.

That difference was explained in medieval thought by a distinction between the use of our mind in the first and in the second intention. We use our minds in the first intention when we use them to know and to understand reality—the world in which we live in all its aspects. We use our minds in the second intention when we use them to know and understand the branches of knowledge that in turn study reality.

Applied to the Propaedia, this distinction requires us to differentiate Part Ten, which has second intentional significance, from Parts One through Nine, which have first intentional significance. Applied to the Syntopicon, the same distinction separates the special set of twelve ideas named from all the rest.

The second volume of the Syntopicon contains an essay on how it was constructed. That essay makes use of this distinction to suggest how ideas in the first intention can be grouped under one or another idea in the second intention. It offers examples of such groupings. These are reported below with some additions that I now think are worth making.

THEOLOGY and RELIGION

Angel, Eternity, God, Immortality, Prophecy, Sin

METAPHYSICS

Being, Cause, Change, Form, God, Infinity, Matter, Necessity and Contingency, One and Many, Opposition, Same and Other, Truth, and perhaps also Quality and Quantity

MATHEMATICS, MECHANICS, PHYSICS

Cause, Chance, Change, Element, Infinity, Matter, Nature, Quality, Quantity, Space, Time, World

LOGIC

Definition, Dialectic, Hypothesis, Induction, Judgment, Language, Opposition, Reasoning, Relation, Rhetoric, Sign and Symbol, Truth, Universal and Particular

POLITICAL THEORY
(Philosophical or Scientific)

Aristocracy, Citizen, Constitution, Custom and Convention, Democracy, Family, Government, Justice, Law, Liberty [and Equality], Monarchy, Oligarchy, Punishment, Revolution, Slavery, State, Tyranny, War and Peace

ETHICS
(or Moral Philosophy)

Courage, Duty, Good and Evil, Happiness, Honor, Justice, Liberty [and Equality], Love, Pleasure and Pain, Prudence, Temperance, Virtue and Vice, Wisdom

ECONOMICS

Labor, Wealth, and also Property (if included)

PSYCHOLOGY
(Philosophical or Scientific)

Animal, Desire, Emotion, Experience, Habit, Knowledge, Language, Love, Man, Memory and Imagination, Mind, Opinion, Pleasure and Pain, Reasoning, Sense, Sign and Symbol, Will

BIOLOGY

Animal, Evolution, Life and Death, Medicine, Sense

The foregoing does not claim to be exhaustive of all the possible ways in which ideas in the first intention can be grouped under ideas in the second intention that are the names of the various branches of knowledge or departments of learning.

There are other ways of grouping ideas—without reference to the disciplines under which they fall. For example, History, Change, Progress, and Time are intimately connected. So, too, are Experience, Habit, Memory and Imagination, and Sense.

Beauty, Good and Evil, and Truth form a traditionally acknowledged triad of fundamental values; so also do Liberty, Equality, and Justice.

The ideas of Knowledge and Opinion belong in a collation with Logic, Mathematics, Metaphysics, Mechanics, Philosophy, Science, and Theology; and with them may be grouped Definition, Hypothesis, Induction, Judgment, Reasoning, and Truth.

The traditionally acknowledged learned professions, which formed the triad of doctoral degrees in medieval universities, are represented in the list of great ideas by Law, Medicine, and Theology. Today we might add Engineering or Technology.

All these groupings of certain great ideas under other great ideas that name familiar disciplines or branches of knowledge, as well as the indication of other ways in which great ideas are interconnected, have much more significance for us than a purely alphabetical listing. They rise above the flat neutrality of the alphabet, but they still do not transcend it to the point where they reach a hierarchical ordering of the ideas in a scale of priorities or of grades of importance.

Whether anything like that can be done in the twentieth century, either for the branches of knowledge or for the great ideas, remains to be seen. Earlier chapters of this book, especially chapters 5 and 6 (which report ancient and medieval schemes for the organization of knowledge), and to some extent even chapters 7, 8, and 9 (which report maps or charts of learning proposed in the seventeenth, eighteenth, and nineteenth centuries), have given us orderings of the parts of knowledge that appeal to philosophical principles, either explicitly or implicitly.

The organization of knowledge, or the ordering and relation of its branches or parts, is essentially a philosophical task. It is not the business of the historian or the scientist. When either historians or scientists attempt to define their own fields of inquiry and to distinguish them from other disciplines, they do so as philosophers, not as historians or scientists.

If any light can be thrown on the problem of how to organize knowledge in the twentieth century—how to order and relate its parts or branches—it must come from philosophy; and it must do so in a manner that accords to some extent with the cultural pluralism and intellectual heterodoxy of the present age.

PART FOUR

PHILOSOPHICAL ILLUMINATION

CHAPTER 13

What Comes Next

I can imagine that some readers who have been patient and persistent enough to reach this point will be somewhat perplexed. They are likely to be wondering what all they have been through adds up to and what comes next.

That state of mind on the part of readers may help me to achieve the objective I had in mind in writing this book.

I have given in the preceding pages a survey of the state of learning in antiquity, in the Middle Ages, and in modern times. In my judgment it was necessary for readers to become acquainted with the traditional maps or charts of learning in those periods, so as to appreciate their need for clarification and their need for guidance as to the state of learning in the contemporary world. *Such guidance is not to be found in the literature of this subject.*

The next chapter will set forth the indispensable insights and distinctions that can be employed in the twentieth century to provide direction and guidance for exploring the whole field of human learning. It will be followed by a conclusion that offers readers guidelines for a lifetime of learning, especially in adult life after all schooling is completed.

[107   ]

The insights and distinctions that constitute the philosophical illuminations to be found in the next chapter are not entirely twentieth-century innovations.

They draw on, or incorporate with modification, Aristotle's hierarchy rising from physics to mathematics and from mathematics to metaphysics in the sphere of theoretical knowledge.

They stress his distinction between the theoretical and the practical spheres of inquiry, with ethics and politics the architectonic disciplines in the practical sphere.

They give a central place to his differentiation of *paideia*, or the general learning that should be in the possession of everyone, from *epistemé*, or the specialized learning that belongs to experts in this or that particular field of knowledge.

They derive insight from the medieval as well as the ancient insistence upon the indispensability of the liberal arts—the skills of the mind involved in every form of inquiry and every process of learning. They derive insight as well from the medieval hierarchy of the three learned professions (medicine, law, and theology), and from the medieval conception of theology as queen of the sciences, with philosophy serving as her handmaiden.

They find additional insight in Francis Bacon's triad of history, poetry, and philosophy, the latter including the empirical and experimental sciences as well as the branches of moral and speculative philosophy, with metaphysics, or *philosophia prima*, at the apex. This is supplemented by Auguste Comte's ordering of the positive sciences and Samuel Taylor Coleridge's plan for a topical encyclopedia.

Putting all these antecedent insights, distinctions, and orderings to good use, in an attempt to do somethig analogous that is appropriate for the twentieth century, it is necessary to separate what is sound from the unsound, and to retain only what is acceptable in the present age.

If readers of this book, reaching this point, have a sense that what they have been offered so far does not give them the guidelines that this work promised to provide, I hope that what lies ahead will fulfill that promise reasonably well.

Information
Knowledge
Understanding
Wisdom
Art
Prudence

CHAPTER 14

Indispensable Insights
and Distinctions

Knowledge < *Prescriptive* —
descriptive —

The Goods of the Mind

AS health, strength, vigor, and vitality are bodily goods, so information, knowledge, understanding, and wisdom are goods of the mind—goods that, acquired, perfect it.

A moment's reflection will discern that these four goods are not coordinate, not of equal value. Rather, as just named, they ascend in a scale of values, information having the least value, wisdom the greatest.

This view of the matter may run against the grain in this age of ours, which we praise for its superabundant information and for the knowledge explosion that distinguishes it from all its predecessors. No one has ever said that it is an age in which understanding has been enlarged or enhanced. Even less would any one dare to say that wisdom has at last come into its own in the twentieth century.

Information—usually acquired bit by bit—is obviously of the least value among the goods of the mind listed above. There is a great deal of useless information, much of it purveyed by newspapers, magazines, and programs on radio and television, and given exaggerated impor-

[110]

tance in a popular game rightly called Trivial Pursuit. There may be some useless knowledge and understanding, but it is difficult to think how that could be; and certainly there is no useless wisdom.

Of course, there is a great deal of useful information, too, but when it is put to use it can be used for either good or evil purposes. Villains, knaves, and scoundrels have to be well-informed to succeed in their nefarious activities. Understanding can seldom be misused; and to speak of a "wise criminal" is a contradiction in terms.

What has just been said about information also applies to knowledge to a certain extent. I am using the word "knowledge" to designate what we might also refer to as a body of knowledge, such as a particular science or a particular branch of philosophy. Unlike information, which comes to us bit by bit, organized knowledge is acquired—or at least put together—in a more systematic fashion. The way in which its component parts are related to one another, their sequence and interconnection, has some intelligible rationale.

There may be no useless knowledge, as there certainly is useless information, but there can be no doubt that knowledge, like information, can be put to good or evil use. Examples of how knowledge applied technologically can be used to the detriment of mankind and even the destruction of civilization are too obvious to need mention. In this century, when we have become acutely aware of this fact, controversy has occurred over the issue of whether a moratorium should be imposed on scientific research that carries with it the promise of technological applications that threaten the future of mankind.

There is another way of perceiving the ascending order in which these four goods of the mind stand. One can have bits of information without having knowledge in the sense defined; and even without possessing a body of knowledge that incorporates such information in its organization. On the other hand, bodies of knowledge— historical, scientific, or philosophical—involve a great deal of information, but always much more than that.

One can have knowledge without understanding the significance of the knowledge possessed, or without understanding its significance as fully as possible. Knowledge accompanied by such understanding is certainly better than bare knowledge in the absence of it; and the greater the understanding that enlightens the knowledge, the better.

Understanding anything presupposes some information or knowledge about it, but not the other way around. Being informed about something or even knowing it does not entail an understanding of it.

Wisdom stands at the top in this sequence of the four goods of the mind It presupposes having the information, knowledge, and understanding requisite for attaining the most fundamental insights that our minds can achieve.

The cultural pluralism and intellectual heterodoxy of the twentieth century may cause us to be intolerant of other hierarchies in the domain of human learning, but it is difficult to see how we could be led to dismiss the ascending scale of values that puts information at the bottom and wisdom at the top, with understood knowledge superior to bare knowledge in the middle. This obviously has a bearing on the value we place upon historical knowledge, the scientific knowledge we possess by means of empirical or experimental research, and the understanding achieved through philosophical reflection about our historical and scientific knowledge.

The Modes of Knowing

If I may now be permitted to use the word "know" in the broadest possible sense, I can translate into other terms the fourfold division of all learning into 1) obtaining or receiving information, 2) acquiring knowledge, 3) supplementing it with understanding, and 4) reaching for wisdom.

First, let it be said that retaining information is an act of memory. Acquiring knowledge, supplementing it with understanding, and attaining wisdom are acts of the intellect and of reason.

We do not need schooling to get information, although far too much of it in fact is devoted to imparting information and not much more. The information that we did not get, or that we have not retained from our schooling, can always be obtained by us in adult life, after our formal education has been completed, through the use of reference books of all sorts—atlases, gazetteers, dictionaries, encyclopedias, and data bases of all sorts.

Schooling should have prepared us to be able to use reference books effectively in order to obtain whatever bits of information we may require. But its much more important function is to prepare us for the growth of our minds in continued learning that enriches our minds not merely with more knowledge than we acquired in school, but with more understanding, and with some approach to wisdom.

Now let us ask what are the modes of knowing when we use the word "know" in the broadest possible sense. Here is the answer: We can *know that, know what, know how, know why* and *wherefore*. Bits of information consist in knowing that something is the case—knowing this particular fact or that one. Beyond knowing facts (that something or other has occurred or exists), we can know what it is, what attributes it has, and in what relations it stands to other things. Historical and scientific knowledge involves knowing *what* as well as *that*. Such knowing requires methodical investigation or research. Knowing *why* and *wherefore* enlightens or illuminates knowing *that* and *what* by insight and understanding and calls for philosophical reflection about whatever it is that we otherwise know. Knowing *why* and *wherefore*, in the most fundamental or ultimate terms, is the attainment of wisdom.

What about knowing how? This takes two forms.* One is knowing how to act for our own good and for the good of the society in which we live. The other is knowing how to make things, how to produce objects that are not to be found in the natural world that surrounds us. These are all works of art, using the word "art" in its broadest sense, meaning, thereby, any productive skill we may have for the production of artifacts.

Within the sphere of art, *know-how* may also consist in the skillful performance of certain activities, such bodily or athletic skills as swimming, skating, skiing, fishing, sailing, dancing, and so on, as well as such intellectual skills as reading, writing, speaking, listening, observing, calculating, measuring, evaluating, estimating, and, of course, thinking.

Used in its broadest sense, the English word "art," which translates the Greek word *"techné,"* covers all these forms of *know-how*. Another Greek word, *phronesis,"* which is translated into English by the word "prudence" or the phrase "practical wisdom," signifies the other kind

---

*Knowing how a machine works is not a form of know-how that consists in a skill we possess.

[114   ]

of *know-how*—knowing how to act for our own good and for the good of the society in which we live.

This can be summarized by saying that one kind of *know-how* consists in the arts or skills of production or performance (for which the Greek word is poiesis, and the other kind of *know-how* consists in the ability to act well and wisely in the conduct of our lives (for which the Greek word is praxis).

Two consequences follow from this consideration of the forms of knowing: we can now add to the four goods of the mind two more goods—the goods named by the words "art" and "prudence"; and giving further consideration to prudence, we now add yet another distinction to those already made with regard to the modes of knowing. Our knowing may be either descriptive and explanatory, or it may be prescriptive and obligatory.

On the one hand, we may know that something is a fact, what it is, and why it is. Then our knowing is descriptive and explanatory. On the other hand, we may know that some objective or goal ought to be sought and that something ought to be done in a certain way or that certain means ought to be chosen to attain the appointed objective or goal. Then our knowing is prescriptive and obligatory.

The two little words "is" and "ought" encapsulate the difference between descriptive and prescriptive knowledge. All our learning would be woefully inadequate for the purposes of life if it were to consist solely in descriptive knowledge.

In both antiquity and in the medieval epoch, one of the most fundamental divisions in the sphere of learning was that between theory and practice—between knowing for the sake of knowing or for the sake of applying knowledge to produce things or to perform well; and knowing for the sake of action, knowing that gives direction to the conduct of our lives and our societies.

The first of these two kinds of knowing is to be found in the division of the sphere of learning that is occupied by history, the empirical sciences and their technological applications, and the branches of speculative philosophy. The second of these two kinds of knowing is to be found in the division of the sphere of learning that is occupied by the branches of practical philosophy: moral and political philosophy.

The superiority of philosophy to history and to the positive or empirical sciences does not lie in its supplying us with more knowledge in the form of *know-that* and *know-what*. It provides us with very little knowledge of that sort as compared with history and science. Nor does such knowledge as philosophy may supply benefit us by giving rise to technological applications or advances. Philosophical knowledge does not have that use: it builds no bridges, bakes no cakes, does not help us *make* anything.

Its superiority lies in its gift of understanding and wisdom—knowledge in the form of *knowing why-and-wherefore*—as well as in the use of such knowledge to give direction to our lives and our societies. This is the prescriptive knowledge to be found in moral and political philosophy.

Epistemé and Paideia

I have used these two Greek words to designate a major division in the sphere of learning, one that comes down to us from antiquity. The word *"epistemé,"* which is translated in Latin by *"scientia,"* signifies all forms of specialized knowledge in which individuals may be expert or competent, some in one specialized field, some

in another, but none in all the diverse forms of specialization that have proliferated in the twentieth century.
Aristotle may have been able to be a competent specialist in all the branches of science that existed in the fourth
century B.C.; but in the twentieth century, the century of
the so-called knowledge explosion, no one can be om-
nicompetent—expert in all specialized departments of
learning.

The word *"paideia,"* which is translated in Latin by
"humanitas," signifies the general learning that should
be in the possession of every human being—learning that
embraces or includes all the ways of knowing that have
been distinguished above.

In using these two Greek words to name two different
approaches to knowledge, I seek to correct a widely
prevalent, mistaken division of learning into the sciences, on the one hand, and the humanities, on the other
hand. I called attention earlier to a misuse of the word
"humanities" that began at the end of the nineteenth
century and has spread since then throughout the academic world.

Wilhelm Dilthey's Germanic bifurcation of all learning
into *Naturwissenschaften* and *Geisteswissenschaften* was
incorrectly turned, in the twentieth century, into the natural (and sometimes the natural and social) sciences, on
the one hand, and the humanities, on the other.

The word "humanities" or the phrase "humanistic
learning" should stand for a generalist approach to all
departments of knowledge, as against a specialist competence in this or that particular branch of knowledge. It
is accordingly incorrect and misleading to identify the
humanities with the branches or departments of knowledge that remain after the various natural and social sciences have been enumerated.

This mistake was made at the University of Chicago in

the 1930s when President Hutchins introduced a four-fold division into the structure of the university, beginning with the 1) physical sciences, 2) the biological sciences, and 3) the social sciences, and ending with 4) the humanities, in order to take care of all the university departments not covered in the first three divisions.

What were "the humanities" in a university thus structured? Philosophy, the study of religion, the study of the fine arts, philology, and the study of foreign languages. Psychology, as a behavioral science, aligned itself with the social sciences; and so did history in part, the remainder aligning itself with the humanities.

In the meaning of the word "humanities" or "humanistic" that I think preserves its original significance as it comes down to us from antiquity and the Middle Ages, any subject that is approached in the manner of the generalist belongs to the humanities or is humanistically approached. A subject that is studied in the manner of the specialist does not belong there.

Mathematics, physics, and biology belong to the humanities when they are examined philosophically in the manner of the generalist. They are then studied humanistically. History, poetry, and philosophy do not belong to the humanities when they are studied in the manner of specialist scholars. They are thus studied, for the most part, by scholars in training for the Ph.D. degree. Such specialized scholarship does not differ essentially from the specialized research in the various departments of empirical science. It is not humanistic.

The word "humanities" should not be used, as it is now generally used in our universities and colleges, and even our high schools, to stand for a particular set of subject matters. Rather it should be used as José Ortega y Gasset used it in his *The Revolt of the Masses,* published in 1930.

That is the book which so eloquently denigrates the barbarism of specialization in the twentieth century, the cultural malady that only the humanities, properly understood, can alleviate.*

The use of the word "philosophy" in the "doctor of philosophy" or Ph.D. degree also deserves comment at this point. Like the word "humanities" as currently misused, "philosophy" is inappropriately applied when we speak of a Ph.D. in physics, in history, in mathematics, in geology, in literature, in music, in chemistry, or in any other university department. This degree is given by all the departments in our university graduate schools that remain after we have set aside the professional schools, and their degrees, such as the J.D. in law, the M.D. in medicine, and the D.D. or S.T.D. in religion or theology.**

The Ph.D. degree, as I have just pointed out, certifies the completion of highly specialized research or scholarship. That is true even when the Ph.D. degree is given in philosophy itself. It does not signify a generalist or humanistic approach to the study of basic ideas. No academic degree now in existence signifies that kind of accomplishment.

The philosopher who conceives philosophy as everybody's business is a generalist, not a specialist. (There are few, if any, academic professors of philosophy who are also philosophers in this sense.) If philosophers are more than just professors of philosophy, they should be encyclopedists who take all fields of learning and all modes of knowing as their province. It follows, of course, that

---

*At the beginning of the century William James anticipated Ortega's insight. He pointed out that any subject can be seen in a humanistic light by being approached historically or philosophically.

**Doctor of Jurisprudence in law, Doctor of Medicine in medicine, and Doctor of Divinity or Doctor of Sacred Theology in religion or theology.

encyclopedists should be philosophers—or humanistic generalists—in the performance of their tasks.*

In our society, and in this century, everyone should be both a generalist and a specialist: a generalist first and last, and a specialist in between. With that in mind, it should be said that the guidance needed in the process of becoming an expert specialist is quite different from the guidance required by those who wish to become cultivated generalists or generally educated human beings.

The alphabetical listing in college and university catalogues of the departments that offer specialized courses of instruction to students who then elect to major in one field and take a minor in another provides the kind of guidance needed by those who wish to specialize. It is totally inadequate for those who may seek something akin to a general education in college and university. They need the kind of direction that I hope this book affords.

Art and Science

7

To achieve the philosophical clarifications I am attempting to provide in this chapter, I am compelled to use words in senses that do not conform to their well-established everyday usages.

Most people use the word "art" for the objects produced by painters and sculptors, which hang on walls or stand on pedestals. If they extend the use of the word to cover more than the visual objects produced by the plastic and graphic arts (thereby including music, poetry, and all forms of imaginative literature, dramatic perfor-

---

*In Appendix II, the reader will find critical passages from *The Revolt of the Masses* and from another book by Ortega also published in 1930, *Mission of the University*. Everything Ortega said about specialization and the specialist in 1930 is many times more applicable to the state of affairs that exists today.

mances, motion pictures, architecture, the ballet, photography, and so on), they still leave unmentioned another large group of artifacts—all the objects produced by the technological applications of the empirical sciences and other crafts, the useful as opposed to the fine arts.

As already indicated, I am asking my readers, for the sake of this clarification of the fields of human learning, to allow me to use the word "art" in its primary sense as the name for a kind of knowing that is a productive skill or a skill of performance—*know-how* as distinct from *know-that, know-what,* and *know-why.*

When the word is thus used no one should have any difficulty in drawing the line that separates art from science, or, stated more precisely, all the arts from all the departments of knowledge that give us *know-that, know-what,* and *know-why,* including here history in all its forms, all the empirical or positive sciences, and all the branches of theoretical philosophy.

The arts as productive *know-how* can also be easily separated from the practical know-how of moral and political philosophy—the *know-how* to act well in the conduct of our lives and our societies.

The Classification of the Arts

In the foregoing paragraphs, I have divided the arts into the fine arts, which produce objects for our enjoyment, and the useful arts, which produce things that can be utilized as means to accomplish whatever purposes technologists and other craftsmen devise them to serve.

In the sphere of the useful arts, we must consider two special groups of skills. One set of skills is traditionally called liberal arts. These are the arts of grammar, rhetoric, and logic—the arts of writing and reading, speaking and listening, and analyzing and interpreting; in short, skill in every form of thinking that employs words.

The liberal arts also include skill in the forms of thinking that employ mathematical symbols instead of ordinary language, and skill in historical research, scientific investigation, and philosophical thought.

The other set of skills in the sphere of the useful arts consists of three arts that are distinguished from all other arts by virtue of the fact that they involve cooperation with nature to help it produce results that would come into existence anyway without human intervention. These are the arts of farming, healing, and teaching. The products of these three arts—food, health, and knowledge (in the broadest sense of that term)—exist or come into existence without the aid of farmers, healers, and teachers.

Farmers, cooperating with nature, help it to produce grains and fruits, and the animals as well as the vegetables we consume as food. Healers, or physicians, cooperating with nature, help the processes whereby animal or human organisms preserve or regain health. Teachers, cooperating with nature, help the activity of learning that goes on in the minds of students in the natural process of acquiring knowledge and understanding. Without such intellectual activity on the part of students, no genuine learning ever occurs, no matter what teachers try to do to make it occur.

All other arts, both fine and useful, produce artificial things, artifacts, or man-made objects—things that would never come into existence naturally or without the intervention of human effort and skill.

The Order of the Sciences

Let us turn now from the classification of the arts to the order of the sciences, using the word "science" for all forms of know-that and know-what.

Here we must first set history apart from all other branches of knowledge by reason of the fact that it deals with particulars, whereas mathematics, the empirical sciences, and the branches of philosophy deal with universals or generalities.

Next, we must distinguish the empirical sciences from mathematics and the branches of philosophy here considered as special departments of knowledge. The former are investigative. They involve observational procedures that obtain the data of special experience, the kind of experience that no one has who does not undertake methodical processes of investigation or inquiry. The latter are noninvestigative.

Mathematicians and philosophers employ experience, but do not need the observational data to be found only in the special experience of investigative empiricists. The experience employed by the mathematician and the philosopher is the common experience of mankind, the experience all of us have in our waking, conscious hours when we are going about our business without using any methods of investigation or engaging in any form of methodical inquiry.*

Like the historian and the empirical scientist, the philosopher as a specialized inquirer is concerned with things or occurrences that exist in reality, whereas the objects of the mathematician do not have real existence. The real existences with which the historian and the empirical scientist are concerned belong to the physical or natural world. That world is also the province of the philosophy of nature, but the philosopher goes beyond that world

---

*The distinctive character of mathematics as just described is exemplified in the history of mathematics from its beginning to the middle of the twentieth century. If in recent years mathematicians have become investigative empiricists, then the character of mathematics in the future may be different.

when, in his metaphysics and theology, he thinks about God and other spiritual beings.

The main division in the sphere of history is between history that is social, political, or economic, and history that is cultural or intellectual.

The ordering of the empirical sciences as physical, biological, and behavioral or social, represents a progression from the simple to the complex, from parts (such as elementary particles, atoms, and molecules) to the wholes they constitute (such as moving bodies studied in terrestrial mechanics and in chemistry, as well as the stars and galaxies studied in astronomy).

We are still going from the simple to the complex when we pass from the physical to the biological sciences and to the study of living organisms. Such disciplines as biophysics, biochemistry, and molecular biology indicate how the sciences that deal with inorganic bodies underlie the sciences that deal with living organisms.

The same step is taken when we pass from all the natural to the social and behavioral sciences. The phenomena with which this group of sciences is concerned—human behavior, human subgroups, and man's social, political, and economic institutions and operations—are still more complex.

The ordering of the empirical sciences just given reflects similar orderings in the nineteenth century by Auguste Comte and Herbert Spencer. The same ordering is to be found in the first five parts of the Propaedia's Outline of Knowledge.

History, Poetry, and Philosophy

We have so far dealt with only two disciplines in Bacon's threefold division of learning into history, poetry, and philosophy. We have considered history and philosophy in relation to one another. But we have not considered poetry in relation to history or poetry in relation to philosophy. It is the latter relationship that is of the greatest importance for us to understand. Beginning with Plato, and continuing through the centuries, the age-old feud between philosophy and poetry deserves pacification.

Like other crucial terms in this discussion, the word "poetry" has a range of meanings stretching from a very broad sense to a narrower one, and to one so limited that it is of little significance for us in this connection. In the broad sense, derived from the Greek word "*poiesis*," poetry stands for all works of fine art with which poetry is akin—music, painting, sculpture, and so on. In a much narrower sense, it means all forms of imaginative literature, not just lyrics, but narrative fiction in both the epic and the dramatic manner (novels and plays), whether written in verse or prose. In the very narrowest sense, poetry is identified with lyrics written in verse. It is this use of the term that can be dismissed.

When Bacon divided the realm of learning into history, poetry, and philosophy, he clearly had in mind poetry as narrative fiction in all its forms. He could not have used poetry to stand for all other works of fine art as well because only imaginative literature, using language as a medium, is comparable to history and philosophy, both of which also use language as a medium of expression.

Bacon was not the first to compare poetry with history and philosophy. Aristotle preceded him, pointing out that poetry is more philosophical than history because, like philosophy and unlike history, it deals with universals.

There is more to it than that. History and philosophy both deal with the actual—history with what has been and philosophy with what is. Philosophy, however, goes beyond the domain of the actual to the much larger realm of the possible. It considers not only what is and must be, but also what can be, but may or may not be.

In this respect poetry is more akin to philosophy than history is, for poetry deals with what can happen, whereas history limits itself to what has happened.

The crucial point of difference between philosophical truth and poetic truth lies in the fact that philosophical truth consists in the conformity of the knowing mind with the way things actually are in reality. Poetic truth is bound only by the limits of the possible, not by the narrower confines of the actual.

Ignoring this difference for the moment, we can now see how closely akin to philosophy poetry is. What Karl von Clausewitz said about the military leader and the diplomat applies to the philosopher and the poet. The latter both seek to achieve the same end, but by different means. Both aim at an understanding of the whole world. Poetry does so without analysis and argument, but with an eloquent use of metaphor, and sometimes with passion; philosophy, by means of analysis and argument, but without metaphorical language and never with passion.

Because they are so closely akin, the rivalry between poetry and philosophy, from Plato's day to the present, has been acute. It can be ameliorated or softened by recognizing that, like analysis and argument, passion pays a role in understanding. Preference for the one rather than the other is a matter of temperament. The fullest understanding involves both.

To put it another way, poetry is an expression of the intellectual imagination; philosophy, an expression of the rational intellect. What is common to them in their gift to us of understanding is their use of the intellect.

We are thus brought to the conclusion that whatever place philosophy occupies in the domain of learning, poetry stands there, too—close by, if not in precisely the same place. Whatever recommendations for the guidance of learning are to be given with regard to philosophy apply to poetry as well.

The Transcendental Forms

Matter and form are inseparably correlative. Matter without form is unintelligible; form without matter is empty. Form gives intelligibility to matter; matter gives content to form.

This insight about form and matter has relevance for us in our consideration of the forms of learning and of the subject matters that they inform, or to which they give form. Are history, science, philosophy (and with it poetry) basic forms, each with various subject matters? Can certain subject matters be common to two or more of these forms; and are certain subject matters capable of taking only one form and not others? Which forms are truly transcendental in the sense of being applicable to all other forms of learning considered as subject matter and, in addition, reflexively applicable to themselves?

Some examples may help to make concretely clear what has just been said so abstractly. We speak of the history of mankind, the science of man and of human behavior, and the philosophy of man. Here *mankind, humanity, human being,* and *human action,* name one and the same subject matter, which can take different forms when human affairs are approached historically, scientifically, and philosophically (or poetically). Similarly, we speak of natural history, natural science, and the philosophy of nature—natural phenomena being the common subject matter of different forms of learning.

We also use such expressions as the history of physics, the science of physics, and the philosophy of physics. The phrase "science of physics" cannot be interpreted in the same way as the phrases "history of physics" and "philosophy of physics." The history of physics is a historical account of the science called physics; so, too, the philosophy of physics is a philosophical understanding of the science called physics. In sharp contrast, the phrase "science of physics" can properly mean only the science that is physics or, as we have just said, the science that is *called* physics.

When physics is considered in the second intention as referring to the discipline itself, but not to its particular subject matter, then there is a history of that discipline and a philosophy of it, but no science of it. Science as a form does not take other disciplines, second-intentionally regarded, as subject matter. The subject matters of all the physical sciences are the phenomena of inorganic nature; the subject matter of all the biological sciences, the phenomena of life and living organisms; the subject matter of the social sciences, societies and social institutions.

Within the realm of the physical sciences we speak of mechanics as the science of bodies in motion, of optics as the science of light, or thermodynamics as the science of heat, and so on. We also speak of the history of mechanics, optics, and thermodynamics. But in that sense of the word "of," we cannot speak of the science of mechanics, the science of optics, or the science of thermodynamics. The meaning of the word "of" is different in the two cases.

In the phrase "history of mechanics," the word "of" has *informative* significance. It means that mechanics as a discipline is the subject matter of the form of learning that is history. In the phrase "science of mechanics," the word "of" does not have *informative* significance. It does not mean that mechanics as a discipline is the subject matter of the form of learning that is science.

There is no scientific approach (as there is a historical and a philosophical approach) to the study of mechanics as a discipline, considered in itself or second intentionally. In the phrase "science of mechanics" the word "of" functions simply as a short way of saying "the science that is mechanics, a study of bodies in motion, which is one of the physical sciences."

How very different from science are history and philosophy as forms of learning. Using the word "of" in a strictly informative sense (relating a form of learning to the subject matters it informs), we can speak of the history of all other forms of learning considered as disciplines in themselves (e.g., the history of science, the history of philosophy or of poetry, the history of mathematics, optics, thermodynamics, and so on). Even further, we can speak reflexively of the history of the discipline that is history itself.

History is thus seen to be a truly transcendental form of learning, both universally applicable to all forms of learning and even reflexively applicable to itself. The same holds true for philosophy. We can speak of the philosophy of other disciplines—the philosophy of history, the philosophy of science, the philosophy of poetry or art, the philosophy of law, the philosophy of medicine. We can also speak reflexively of the philosophy of philosophy itself.

In all the foregoing uses of the phrase "philosophy of," what is connoted can be expressed by the phrase "understanding of." The same connotation explains the phrase "philosophy of philosophy" when the form of learning that is philosophy is applied reflexively to philosophy itself as a discipline.

Science falls far short of being a transcendental form like history and philosophy. There is certainly no science of science—no scientific approach to the study of science as a discipline in itself. Nor is there a science of history, as there is a history and a philosophy of science. If the phrase "science of history" is to be given any meaning at all, it can only have reference to the use of something akin to scientific method in historical investigations.

There can be no science of philosophy as there can be a philosophy of science—no scientific study of philosophy as there can be a philosophical understanding of science. We are hard put to find any meaningful interpretation of the phrase "science of philosophy."

As truly transcendental forms of learning, history and philosophy (and with it poetry) are coordinate with one another. Science, not being a transcendental form of learning, is not coordinate with them. However, science is a basic form of learning even if it is not a transcendental form. How, then, does science fit into the picture of all the basic forms of learning, transcendental or not?

The answer lies in the fact that science and philosophy as forms of learning do have certain subject matters in common, principally the phenomena of nature; human beings and their behavior; the human mind, its acts and processes; human society, its institutions and arrangements. In other words, we have both natural science and a philosophy of nature; scientific and philosophical anthropology; scientific psychology and a philosophy of mind; the social sciences and social or political philosophy.

Science and philosophy part company with respect to certain subject matters. Such subjects as light and heat in the realm of physical phenomena belong only to science. So, too, do such subject matters as cells, digestion,

and the nervous system in the realm of biological phenomena; and such subject matters as economic transac-
tions and mob behavior in the realm of social phenomena.
They belong only to science.

Understanding this point is so important that I wish to
make it clear in another way. There is a physics of light
(the science that is called optics). There is a physics of
heat (the science that is called thermodynamics). We can,
therefore, also speak of a science of light and a science
of heat. But there is no history of light or heat, no philosophy of light or heat.

In short, when the subject matter is a special area of
natural or social phenomena, we can, with a few exceptions, have a science of that special subject matter, but
not a history or philosophy of it.* What we can have is
a history or philosophy of this or that discipline which
consists in the scientific study of that particular subject
matter.

The subject matters that belong only to philosophy are
the subject matter of metaphysics (as treating being or
existence in all its modes and the properties of each
mode), and the subject matter of theology (as treating God
and other spiritual beings).

There is still another point at which science and philosophy as forms of learning part company. Science as a
form of learning consists entirely of descriptive knowledge—knowledge of what is or happens. When we come
to the phenomena of human behavior, individually and
socially, science gives us knowledge of how men do in
fact behave individually and how they do in fact conduct themselves socially and carry on their social life. As

---

* The few exceptions that come to mind are the Earth and mankind. We can
have a history of the Earth and of mankind, as well as a science of the Earth
and of man. We can also have a philosophical anthropology.

contrasted with the descriptive knowledge to be found in the various behavioral and social sciences, we must turn to the prescriptive knowledge to be found in moral and political philosophy. It is this which gives us an understanding of how men ought to conduct their individual and social lives, or why they should behave in one way rather than another.

In this account of the four basic forms of learning (history, science, and philosophy together with poetry), no mention has been made of mathematics. It is certainly a form of learning by virtue of the fact that there are diverse branches of mathematics, each with its own subject matter (arithmetic, algebra, geometry, calculus, topology, and so on). It is just as certainly not a transcendental form. As a discipline considered in itself, there is a history of mathematics and a philosophy of mathematics, but no science of mathematics. The phrase "science of mathematics" simply means the science that is mathematics, or the mathematical sciences as a group.

The word "science" is used appropriately here, for mathematics is much more akin to all the natural sciences than it is to philosophy. It gives us the kind of knowledge that consists of *know-that* and *know-what*, and even *know-how* (the mathematical skills), but not the kind of knowledge that consists of *know-why-and-wherefore*.

On the other hand, mathematics does have some kinship with philosophy in that the objects of pure mathematics belong to the realm of the possible, as do some of the objects of philosophy. Of these objects, some enter into the realm of the actual when mathematics is applied in the physical, biological, and social sciences. The fact that mathematics can be applied in the sphere of science, but not in the spheres of history and philosophy, associates mathematics with science as a form of learning, a form of learning that is basic but not transcendental.

Finally, what about logic? We have already discussed logic as a liberal art—a skill that is involved in all forms of learning. There is, of course, a history of logic and a philosophy of logic, but not a science of logic (except in the sense expressed by the phrase "the science that is called logic").

One view of logic as a science, not an art, associates it closely with mathematics or makes it continuous with mathematics. In another view of logic as a science, it is either pure or applied. Pure logic was traditionally called formal logic, and the applications of logic were called material logic.

Formal logic is concerned with the elements, principles, and rules or laws of thought. Material logic consists of the application of these principles and rules to various branches of knowledge. It can also be thought of as their methodology.

There is a logic or methodology of history, of science, and of philosophy (but not of poetry). In the sphere of science, there are different methodologies for diverse particular sciences, certainly a different methodology in the natural sciences, on the one hand, and in the social sciences, on the other hand. In the sphere of philosophy, the logic or methodology of its speculative (or descriptive) branches, such as the philosophy of nature and metaphysics, is different from the logic or methodology of its practical (or prescriptive) branches, such as ethics and politics. Thinking about what is, what can be, and what must be differs from thinking about what ought or ought not to be sought and done.

The view of logic that makes it continuous with mathematics gives logic the same place in the realm of learning that mathematics occupies, a place that is adjunct to the place occupied by the natural and social sciences. Like the sciences to which it is adjunct, it is a basic form of learning but not transcendental.

The other view of logic as a science, both pure and applied, changes its status. Since it is applicable to all other forms of learning (that is, all except poetry), it would appear to have something akin to a transcendental character. Yet it falls short of that, for it is not reflexively applicable to itself, as history and philosophy are. There is no logic of logic.

CHAPTER 15

Recapitulation: An Aide-Mémoire for the Reader

OF the philosophical insights and distinctions set forth in the preceding chapter, what should readers bear in mind as they turn now to the guidelines for a lifetime of learning that they will find in the Conclusion to follow? Here are twelve points to remember.

1. *The four goods of the mind—information, organized knowledge, understanding, and wisdom—arranged in an ascending scale of values.* That wisdom is the supreme good of the human mind explains why this guidebook to learning is for a lifelong pursuit of wisdom.

2. *The fourfold differentiation of knowing into 1) know-that, 2) know-what, 3) know-how, and 4) know-why-and-wherefore.* Of these, the first two dominate the domains of history, empirical science, and mathematics. The second and fourth belong to philosophy. The third to art and prudence, which are two additional goods of the mind in its productive and practical operations.

3. *The distinction between a) epistemé and b) paideia, i.e., between a) the specialized knowledge or skill of the expert in some particular field of subject matter, and b) the general learning and the intellectual skills that should be the possession of every human being.*

4. *The misconception of the humanities when they are*

regarded *as whatever subject matters are not covered by
the natural and social sciences.* Any intellectual discipline and any field of learning belongs to the humanities
when it is philosophically approached in the manner of
the generalist for the sake of becoming a generally educated human being.

5. *The misuse of the word "philosophy" in the Ph.D.
degree to certify the acquirement of specialized competence in any field of subject matter outside the domains
of such professional disciplines as law, medicine, and
theology.* The Ph.D. degree can be earned for specialized
competence in some branch of philosophical scholarship, but no academic degree honors a philosophical understanding of basic ideas and issues.

6. *The difference between art (both fine and useful arts)
and science (and other fields of research or scholarship)
involving the difference between productive know-how
and descriptive know-that, know-what, and know-why-
and-wherefore.*

7. *The distinction between a) descriptive and explanatory truth, and b) prescriptive and obligatory truth; or
between a) knowing that which is, what it is, and why it
is, and b) knowing what ought to be sought and what
ought to be done to attain it.* Only moral and political
philosophy gives us knowledge of the goals we ought to
seek and the means we ought to choose in order to achieve
those goals.

8. *The division of the arts into the fine arts or the en-
joyable arts of the beautiful; and the useful arts that
supply us with tools, instruments, and other utilities.* The
arts called liberal are among the useful arts, comprising
all the intellectual skills we need to use language effectively, to learn anything, and to think about anything.

9. *The association of poetry, including all forms of
imaginative literature, with philosophy humanistically*

conceived *as the generalist approach to all subject mat-*
ters in the light of basic ideas. They are akin in the benefits they confer upon us though they differ in the means
they employ to do so. They both give us an understanding of the world and of ourselves, and insight into the
human condition without which little wisdom can be
gained. Poetry enlightens us by intellectual vision without analysis and argument, but with eloquent language,
the use of metaphors, and sometimes with passion. Philosophy enriches our understanding by clarity in analysis and argument, but eschews metaphorical language and
avoids passion.

10. *The primacy of the roles played by poetry and*
philosophy in a lifelong pursuit of wisdom. Along with
history, they are the transcendental forms of learning,
applicable to all the objects with which the human mind
is concerned.

11. *The secondary importance of all other disciplines*
which, though basic, are not transcendental forms of
learning. As fields of specialization, these include all the
empirical sciences, the mathematical sciences, and other
branches of scholarship. They also include historical research and philosophical scholarship as fields of specialization.

12. *The transformation of specialized disciplines into*
matters appropriate for general education by a human-
istic approach to them. Any and every field of specialization becomes of significance to the generalist in the light
thrown upon it by the history or philosophy of it.

As we shall see in the Conclusion to follow, those who
wish to become specialists in some particular discipline
or subject matter should concentrate on some division of
mathematics or empirical science, some branch of historical research, or some branch of philosophical scholarship.

Those who wish, in addition, to become generally educated human beings should give primacy to the humanistic or generalist approach to all disciplines or subject matters, with the understanding of them that is conferred by history, philosophy, and poetry as the transcendental forms of learning.

Conclusion:
Paideia for the
Autodidact

LET me translate into intelligible, and somewhat expanded, English the briefer Greek in the title of this conclusion: a guide to *general* learning for those who, after completing their schooling in youth, aspire to become generally educated human beings by the self-conducted learning they carry on in adult life.

The first point of emphasis is indicated by the word "general," which as already pointed out is in the connotation of the Greek word *"paideia"* and its Latin equivalent *"humanitas."* Those who wish only to become specialists—to become experts in this or that field of knowledge or to become competent in one or another skill—do not need this, or any other, guidebook to learning.

If they have no interest in becoming generally educated, basic schooling as it now exists, and colleges and universities as they are now structured, will suffice for their purposes.

This is especially true of our colleges and universities. Their catalogues, listing one department after another in alphabetical order, offer an array of courses in which individuals can elect to specialize, in a major and a minor way, according to their tastes and interests. It is even true of our high schools, for as now structured they, too, offer an extraordinary array of elective opportunities for premature specialization.

I said earlier in this book that, ideally, everyone should be both a generalist and a specialist—a generalist first at the level of basic schooling (K through 12), and also last in the years after college and university, with becoming a specialist intermediate between these two stages of one's education. That intermediate stage of specialization occupies the years spent in college and university.

The program of learning just outlined is the Paideia ideal, by which I mean the ideal set forth in three books that I wrote or edited for twenty or more educators in the Paideia group of which I was chairman. The books are: *The Paideia Proposal* (1982), *Paideia Problems and Possibilities* (1983), and *The Paideia Program* (1984).

If the Paideia ideal were now being actualized in the elementary and secondary schools of this country, the first two steps in the program would be realized. Schooling from kindergarten through grade 12 would initiate the young in the process of acquiring general, liberal, and humanistic learning. The colleges and universities to which some of them then went would afford them opportunity for specialization in a field or fields that they elected to pursue.

If, when they completed their institutional education, they realized, as everyone should, that they had not completed their education, they would continue learning in their adult years. Such continued learning should, of course, be general, not specialized, if they have any hope of becoming generally educated human beings at the end of life.

Since the Paideia program, as outlined in the third Paideia book, describes the content of general learning in the first stage of institutional education, the present guidebook need be concerned only with the third stage of general learning—the stage where the learning is self-conducted by the mature person who functions as an autodidact (i.e., one who is self-educated).

Unfortunately for those to whom this book is addressed, whether they be young or old, the Paideia ideal is very far from being realized at present. Of what advantages have they been deprived by this sad fact?

They have been deprived of three things, of which the first is most important.

1) They have not acquired the liberal arts, the skills of learning that are indispensable for their pursuit of learning, both in educational institutions and thereafter. I have already enumerated these skills as the four language arts of reading, writing, speaking, and listening; the skills involved in mathematical operations; the skills in the various procedures of the empirical and experimental sciences, and more generally the skills operative in thinking about any subject matter.

2) They have not had the occasion to make a sufficient initial acquaintance with imaginative literature and other fine arts, with mathematics as a science, with the natural sciences, and with history, geography, and social studies. Their acquaintance with these fields of learning will have been spotty and inadequate. The information they acquired in order to pass examinations will soon have been forgotten. This defect need not be remedied since, in later life, they can obtain whatever information they want at one time or another by recourse to reference books of all sorts.

3) The third deprivation they will have suffered is the absence from their early schooling of an initial enhancement of their understanding by the discussion of basic ideas and issues in seminars that should occur in all twelve grades from kindergarten on. That initial growth

of their understanding, if it were to occur, would hardly be adequate. That most important aspect of their education should be continued in college and university as a foundation for the general learning to be pursued in all the later years of life.

To achieve this, our colleges and the graduate or professional schools of our universities need not supplant the diverse forms of specialized education they now offer by substituting truly general education at this higher level. They need only supplement and ameliorate that specialized education by adding to it the continuation of the kind of learning and teaching that involves the enhancement of the understanding. This could be done by requiring all students at this higher level to participate in seminars in which basic ideas and issues are discussed, regardless of which field of specialization they are pursuing.

The facts being as they are, our schools, colleges, and universities are not now turning out specialists who *also* have been initiated into the process of becoming generally educated. If their graduates are to become generally educated human beings in the course of their lives, that will have to be accomplished by their undertaking it for themselves as autodidacts. What little training they have received in the liberal arts, or skills of learning, will have to be supplemented by their own efforts to improve their ability to read, write, speak, and listen effectively and, in general, to think effectively.

Given this state of affairs as probably irremediable in the immediate future, I will now try to summarize what this guide book to learning offers in the way of direction and guidance for those who still wish to become generally educated, in spite of all the deficiencies in their institutional education.

As far as the arts are concerned, and apart from the

liberal skills that everyone must make an effort to develop, the pursuit of general learning should involve some experience of, and the formation of good taste with regard to, the objects produced by as many of the fine arts as possible. Individuals may become specialists in one or another of these departments of fine art, but that is not requisite for their general education. What is especially necessary is the continuation throughout life of the kind of learning, the kind of understanding that poetry or imaginative literature affords.

In addition to this requirement, the other two forms of learning, coordinate with learning from poetry, are learning by the reading of histories and biographies and by the reading of philosophical books, intended for the layman and dealing with great ideas and issues. The branches of philosophical knowledge taught in our colleges and universities are not to the point here. They are not intended for the layman and they seldom deal with great ideas and issues. As taught and learned in our colleges and universities, they have become fields of intense specialization, no different in this respect from the intense specialization that goes on in logic, mathematics, the various positive sciences, and the branches of technology.

So far I have named all of the transcendental forms of learning as components in the self-education of adults who wish to become generally educated human beings. All these should be pursued under the auspices of philosophy, meaning thereby that they should be pursued primarily for the purpose of enlarging one's understanding of physical nature, human nature, and human society.

What about the particular positive or empirical sciences? They enter into continuing self-education that is generalist rather than specialist in its approach to everything only to the extent that some understanding of these disciplines and their subject matters should be a part of everyone's general education. In the case of the particular empirical sciences, as in the case of history, the learning to be done should be philosophical in its approach—for the sake of understanding the world better, not for the sake of achieving the competence of an expert. That, in the twentieth century, would be impossible for anyone to achieve with respect to all the disciplines and subject matters mentioned.

What, then, shall autodidacts do? How should persons proceed who wish to conduct for themselves the continuation of learning after all schooling has been finished?

The answer is in one way very brief and simple. Looked at another way it is rich and substantial enough to occupy a lifetime of learning in the pursuit of wisdom.

The simple answer is: *Read and discuss!* Never just read, for reading without discussion with others who have read the same book is not nearly as profitable as it should be for the mind in its effort to understand what has been read. As reading without discussion can fail to yield the full measure of understanding that should be sought, so discussion without the substance for discussion that good and great books afford is likely to degenerate into chitchat or be little more than an exchange of opinions and personal prejudices.

I have written two books that should prove helpful to anyone who obeys the injunction to read and discuss. *How to Read a Book*, published in 1940 and still currently available in a revised edition in paperback, originally carried the subtitle "The Art of Getting a Liberal Education." Chapter 21 in that book is entitled "Reading and the Growth of the Mind."

More recently, I wrote *How to Speak/How to Listen*, published in 1983 and now available in paperback. After setting forth rules that, if followed, make serious discussion both profitable and pleasant, it contains a concluding chapter on the importance of conversation in human life for the growth of the mind in its pursuit of understanding and wisdom.

Beyond the simple answer—*Read and discuss*—lies the richer answer, the answer to the question: *What should be read and discussed?* That answer I have tried to provide in Appendix III, entitled "Some Books That May Be Helpful to Autodidacts."

There I have recommended a relatively small number of great books of poetry, history, and philosophy, books which provide the substance for discussion of great ideas and issues.

For those who wish to go further, and especially for those who wish to supplement the great books in the tradition of Western thought by reading important contemporary works, I have suggested two books that comment on such works as well as on the great works of the past. In addition, I have mentioned other books of my own, philosophical books about ideas, books intended for the layman, not for professors of philosophy.

If the prescriptions laid down above are followed, what picture shall we paint to portray the ultimate result? What would generally educated human beings be like?

They would have sufficient acquaintance with science and history to give them the knowledge they need to understand the world of nature and of man. For that knowledge to be *understood* knowledge, not just *bare* knowledge, it would have to be enlightened by poetry and philosophy. All this knowledge and the understanding of it should ultimately lead to the attainment of some modicum of wisdom, both practical and theoretical.

In this picture, philosophy and, with it, poetry have a certain primacy. One reason for this is that the questions they raise for us and help us to answer are more important for our lives than the questions raised and answered by all other disciplines. This is especially true in the realm of moral and political philosophy—questions about what goals ought to be sought and what ought to be done to achieve them, in the conduct of individual lives, in the direction of human society, and in the improvement of its institutions.

One other reason for the primacy of philosophy is the role it plays in relation to religion. The history of diverse religions and the comparative study of them do not suffice for those among us who feel that their lives are incomplete without a religious aspect or without participation in a religious community.

For this, a philosophical understanding of religion is required. Borrowing from the sense in which the Middle Ages regarded philosophy as the handmaiden of theology, I think it can be said in the twentieth century that philosophy in general and philosophical theology in particular lead to the boundary line that separates the realm of natural knowledge, based on human experience and reason, from the realm of faith in revealed truth, which is supernatural knowledge. It takes a leap of faith to cross that boundary line, but that leap cannot be taken, or will be taken blindly, unless one has reached that boundary line in the course of learning. Philosophy, not history or science, enables one to get there.

With the picture of the generally educated human being before our eyes, what test or measure can anyone use to have some assurance that the goal has been achieved with some degree of approximation, never perfectly of course?

There are undoubtedly many ways of answering this question. I have one to propose. I think the mark or measure of a generally educated human being is that the individual should feel comfortably at home in the whole realm of human learning.

Another way of saying this is that individuals should be able to examine the Propaedia's synoptic Outline of Knowledge (see Appendix I) and find nothing there that totally escapes his understanding. They should also be able to examine the Syntopicon's list of the great ideas and the account of their grouping into subsets (see pp. 96–104), and also feel competent to ask intelligent questions about all of them and to engage in a discussion of the issues they raise.

The Propaedia's Synoptic Outline of Knowledge*

Part One.   Matter and Energy

Division I. Atoms: Atomic Nuclei and Elementary Particles
     111.   The Structure and Properties of Atoms
     112.   The Atomic Nucleus and Elementary Particles

Division II. Energy, Radiation, and the States and Transformation of Matter
     121.   Chemical Elements: Periodic Variation in Their Properties
     122.   Chemical Compounds: Molecular Structure and Chemical Bonding
     123.   Chemical Reactions
     124.   Heat, Thermodynamics, and the Nonsolid States of Matter
     125.   The Solid State of Matter
     126.   Mechanics of Particles, Rigid Bodies, and Deformable Bodies: Elasticity, Vibrations, and Flow

---

*This synoptic outline presents only the forty-two divisions and the 186 sections of the Propaedia's ten parts. Each of these 186 sections is further subdivided into a number of topics, which represent an analysis of the subject matter covered in that section of the outline. The complete outline of knowledge—its ten parts, its forty-two divisions, its 186 sections, and its thousands upon thousands of topics—occupies 760 pages in the Propaedia.

Part Four.   Human Life

Part Five.   Human Society

Division II. Social Organization and Social Change
    521. Social Structure and Change
    522. The Group Structure of Society
    523. Social Status
    524. Human Populations: Urban and Rural Communities

Division III. The Production, Distribution, and Utilization of Wealth
    531. Economic Concepts, Issues, and Systems
    532. The Consumer and the Market: Pricing and the Mechanisms for Distributing Goods
    533. The Organization of Production and Distribution
    534. The Distribution of Income and Wealth
    535. Macroeconomics
    536. Economic Growth and Planning

Division IV. Politics and Government
    541. Political Theory
    542. Political Institutions: the Structure, Branches, and Offices of Government
    543. The Functioning of Government: the Dynamics of the Political Process
    544. International Relations: Peace and War

Division V. Law
    551. Philosophies and Systems of Law; the Practice of Law
    552. Branches of Public Law, Substantive and Procedural
    553. Branches of Private Law, Substantive and Procedural

Division VI. Education
    561. The Aims and Organization of Education
    562. Education Around the World

Part Six.   Art

Part Seven.   Technology

944. Central Africa to *c.* 1885
945. Southern Africa to *c.* 1885

Division V. Peoples and Civilizations of Pre-Columbian
    America
951. Andean Civilization to *c.* A.D. 1540
952. Meso-American Civilization to *c.* A.D. 1540

Division VI. The Modern World to 1920
961. Western Europe from *c.* 1500 to *c.* 1789
962. Eastern Europe, Southwest Asia, and North
    Africa from *c.* 1480 to *c.* 1800
963. Europe from 1789 to *c.* 1920
964. European Colonies in the Americas from 1492
    to *c.* 1790
965. Development of the United States and Canada
    from 1763 to 1920
966. Development of the Latin-American and Carib-
    bean Nations to *c.* 1920
967. Australia and Oceania to *c.* 1920
968. South Asia under the Influence of European
    Imperialism from *c.* 1500 to *c.* 1920
969. Southeast Asia Under the Influence of Euro-
    pean Imperialism to *c.* 1920
96/10. China from 1839 Until the Onset of Revolu-
    tion (to *c.* 1911), and Japan from the Meiji
    Restoration to *c.* 1910
96/11. Southwest Asia and North Africa (*c.* 1800–
    1920), and Sub-Saharan Africa (1885–
    c. 1920) Under the Influence of European
    Imperialism: the Early Colonial Period

Division VII. The World Since 1920
971. International Movements, Diplomacy, and War
    Since 1920
972. Europe Since *c.* 1920
973. The United States and Canada Since 1920
974. Latin-American and Caribbean Nations Since
    c. 1920

975. East Asia: China in Revolution, the Era of Japanese Hegemony, and the Influence of the United States in the Twentieth Century
976. South and Southeast Asia: the Late Colonial Period and the Emergence of New Nations Since 1920
977. Australia and Oceania Since 1920
978. Southwest Asia and Africa: the Late Colonial Period and the Emergence of New Nations in the Twentieth Century

Part Ten.   The Branches of Knowledge

Division I. Logic
    10/11. History and Philosophy of Logic
    10/12. Formal Logic, Metalogic, and Applied Logic

Division II. Mathematics
    10/21. History and Foundations of Mathematics
    10/22. Branches of Mathematics
    10/23. Applications of Mathematics

Division III. Science
    10/31. History and Philosophy of Science
    10/32. The Physical Sciences
    10/33. The Earth Sciences
    10/34. The Biological Sciences
    10/35. Medicine and Affiliated Disciplines
    10/36. The Social Sciences and Psychology
    10/37. The Technological Sciences

Division IV. History and the Humanities
    10/41. Historiography and the Study of History
    10/42. The Humanities and Humanistic Scholarship

Division V. Philosophy
    10/51. History of Philosophy
    10/52. The Nature and the Divisions of Philosophy
    10/53. Philosophical Schools and Doctrines

Appendix II

Ortega on the Barbarism of Specialization

[The scientist who] is only acquainted with one science, and even of that one only knows the small corner in which he is an active investigator . . . even proclaims it as a virtue that he takes no cognisance of what lies outside the narrow territory specially cultivated by himself, and gives the name of "dilettantism" to any curiosity for the general scheme of knowledge.

Anyone who wishes can observe the stupidity of thought, judgment, and action shown today in politics, art, religion, and the general problems of life and the world by the "men of science," and, of course, behind them, the doctors, engineers, financiers, teachers, and so on.

Compared with the medieval university, the contemporary university has developed the mere seed of professional instruction into an enormous activity; it has added the function of research; and it has abandoned almost entirely the teaching or transmission of culture.

[The citizen] is the new barbarian. . . . This new barbarian is above all the professional man, more learned than ever before, but at the same time more uncultured—the engineer, the physician, the lawyer, the scientist.

"General culture." The absurdity of the term, its Philistinism, betrays its insincerity. "Culture," referring to the human mind and not to stock or crops, cannot be anything else but general. There is no being "cultured" in physics or mathematics. That would mean simply to be *learned* in a particular subject. The usage of the expression "general culture" shows an underlying notion that the student ought to be given some ornamental knowledge, which in some way is to educate his moral character or his intellect. For so vague a purpose, one discipline is as good as another, among those that are more or less indefinite and not so technical—like philosophy, or history, or sociology!

Civilization has had to await the beginning of the twentieth century, to see the astounding spectacle of how brutal, how stupid, and yet how aggressive is the man learned in one thing and fundamentally ignorant of all else. Professionalism and specialism, through insufficient counterbalancing, have smashed the European man in pieces; and he is consequently missing at all the points where he claims to be, and is badly needed.

Let us cast away once [and] for all those vague notions of enlightenment and culture, which make them appear as some sort of ornamental accessory for the life of leisure. There could not be a falser misrepresentation. Culture is an indispensable element of life, a dimension of our existence, as much a part of man as his hands; . . . but that is no longer simply man: it is man crippled. The same is to be said of life without culture, only in a much more fundamental sense. It is a life crippled, wrecked, false. The man who fails to live at the height of his times is living beneath what would constitute his right life. Or in other words, he is swindling himself out of his own life.

Some Books That May Be Helpful to Autodidacts

I have divided my recommendations into three parts. The first set, **A,** concerns works of imaginative literature, history or biography, and philosophy. The second, **B,** mentions three "how-to" books that I have written about the liberal arts. The third, **C,** also recommends some books of mine about the great ideas.

A

Great Books of the Western World (54 volumes)

Of the seventy-four authors included in this set of books, I recommend as a starter the following relatively short list.

Homer: *The Iliad, The Odyssey*
Sophocles: *Antigone, Oedipus Rex*
Thucydides: *The History of the Peloponnesian War*
Plato: *The Apology, The Republic*
Aristotle: *Ethics, Politics*
Tacitus: *The Annals*
Plutarch: *The Lives of the Noble Grecians and Romans*
Augustine: *Confessions*
Dante: *The Divine Comedy*
Cervantes: *Don Quixote*
Montaigne: *Essays*

Philosophical Illumination

Machiavelli: *The Prince*
Pascal: *Pensées*
Shakespeare: *Hamlet, Macbeth, Othello, King Lear*
Adam Smith: *The Wealth of Nations*
Edward Gibbon: *The Decline and Fall of the Roman Empire*
Jonathan Swift: *Gulliver's Travels*
J. S. Mill: *Representative Government*
Tolstoy: *War and Peace*
Melville: *Moby Dick*
William James: *The Principles of Psychology*

To supplement the foregoing, I suggest two much more far-ranging lists of recommended readings that include outstanding books written in the twentieth century.

Clifton Fadiman: *Lifetime Reading Plan*
Charles Van Doren: *The Joy of Reading*

B

How to Read a Book (the second edition, in the writing of which Charles Van Doren was my collaborator)
How to Speak/How to Listen
The Paideia Program (which contains essays by other members of the Paideia group as well as by me)

C

Six Great Ideas
A Vision of the Future: Twelve Ideas for a Better Life and a Better Society
How to Think About God
Ten Philosophical Mistakes

Some Books That May Be Helpful to Autodidacts

Here I would also recommend the 102 essays on the great ideas that I wrote for the Syntopicon, which is included in *Great Books of the Western World.*